IN A LANDSCAPE REDRAWN

Published 2017 by
Veritas Publications
7–8 Lower Abbey Street
Dublin 1, Ireland
publications@veritas.ie
www.veritas.ie

ISBN 978 1 84730 774 3

Copyright © Donal Murray, 2017

10 9 8 7 6 5 4 3 2 1

The material in this publication is protected by copyright law. Except as may be permitted by law, no part of the material may be reproduced (including by storage in a retrieval system) or transmitted in any form or by any means, adapted, rented or lent without the written permission of the copyright owners. Applications for permissions should be addressed to the publisher.

A catalogue record for this book is available from the British Library.

Designed by Padraig McCormack, Veritas Publications
Printed in Ireland by SPRINT-print Ltd, Dublin

Veritas books are printed on paper made from the wood pulp of managed forests. For every tree felled, at least one tree is planted, thereby renewing natural resources.

IN A LANDSCAPE REDRAWN

Bishop Donal Murray

VERITAS

Contents

Introduction   7

Chapter One
Who are We?   11

Chapter Two
A Meagre Awareness   31

Chapter Three
Redrawing the Landscape   43

Chapter Four
Conscience: On Not Being Judgemental   61

Chapter Five
What is the Question?   77

Chapter Six
Mutual Incomprehension   99

Chapter Seven
To Sum Up: All is Gift   125

Endnotes   147

Introduction

There has always been an enigma about the relationship of Christian faith to the world in which it lives. Sometimes faith existed as a predominant and widely respected aspect of life; sometimes it has succumbed to the temptation to act as if it were a government. Sometimes it has existed in an atmosphere which is downright hostile; sometimes in an atmosphere that is merely uncomfortable. Sometimes the surrounding society is completely uncomprehending and regards faith as irrelevant and doomed to extinction. One can see elements of each of these in our time. Perhaps the context most damaging to faith is the first one, where believers are tempted to feel complacent about themselves and about the future of faith in the world. Thankfully, that temptation is much less prevalent today than in the past.

This book seeks to look at our situation from the point of view of two questions. In the first place it seeks to reflect on the question of who we human beings are, the meaning and purpose of our lives, and how Christian faith illuminates our nature and dignity.

The second question is about how we understand our freedom and how we make moral decisions. This is an area where dramatic changes in our cultural situation are obviously occurring. Actions which were universally regarded as wrong, and sometimes as criminal, are increasingly regarded as fundamental rights. Rabbi Jonathan Sacks, one of the most perceptive commentators on the contemporary world, speaks of 'a profound redrawing or our moral landscape'.[1]

The two questions are intimately linked. How people should behave depends on what one believes a person to be and what one understands as the purpose of human life – that is if one recognises any overall purpose of life. Any culture's way of approaching moral questions follows from how people regard human beings and what they see as the meaning and source of their human dignity. The same can be said of how we formulate social policy, and of how we regard the role of education and health care. How individuals and society as a whole approach these issues says more than we may think about how they understand themselves and the goal of human life.

Human life *has* a goal. For those who believe the Good News of Christ, we not only *have* a goal, we *are* a quest for the fulfilment that we cannot provide for ourselves. In religious terms we say, with St Augustine, that our hearts are restless until they rest in God.[2] That restlessness is always present, even if it is not expressed in religious language. Every human being experiences longings that are never completely fulfilled. Christians see such longings as the fruit of having been invited by the Creator into a fulfilment beyond imagining, a fulfilment which can only be a gift of God. That invitation is never withdrawn, however determinedly one tries to ignore it.

The two questions intersect: 'who are we?' and 'how do we understand our freedom and our choices?' Individual free actions always have some relationship to the first question. They are either steps towards the fulfilment of our quest or they are not.

But this ordering to one's ultimate end is not something merely subjective, dependent solely upon one's intention. It presupposes that such acts are in themselves capable of being ordered to that end, insofar as they are in conformity with the authentic moral good of [the human being] safeguarded by the commandments. This is what Jesus himself points out in his reply to the young man: 'If you wish to enter into life, keep the commandments.'[3]

Chapter One

Who are We?

The first question, therefore, to be asked in reflecting on moral issues is: 'who are we? What is a human being?' Without addressing that question, we cannot hope to say anything that would make sense about how human beings should behave.

Pope John Paul said in his first encyclical that when we seek to understand ourselves in the light of the mystery of Christ this gives rise not only to adoration of God but to deep wonder at ourselves.[1] The name for that deep amazement, he said, is the Gospel.

When he spoke about what he called 'the fundamental questions that pervade human life', he began with these:

> *Who am I? Where have I come from and where am I going? Why is there evil? What is there after this life?* ... [These] are questions which have their common source in the quest for meaning which has always compelled the human heart. In fact, the answer given to these questions decides the direction which people seek to give to their lives.[2]

Such questions are found in some form in religions, philosophies and in all the various ways in which people search for meaning: in art, in literature, in science, in political action, in contemplation.

Although we may think we are too busy to reflect on them, these are questions which, even when ignored, continue to lie deep in the human heart. They can be awakened by the shattering of hope, by personal disillusionment, by natural disasters, by bereavement; they can also arise from experiences of love and joy, of wonder at the immensity of the universe and of being overwhelmed by the beauty that surrounds us.

The first chapter of the Book of Genesis describes who we are:

> Then God said, '*Let us make humankind in our image, according to our likeness*; and let them have dominion over the fish of the sea, and over the birds of the air, and over the cattle, and over all the wild animals of the earth, and over every creeping thing that creeps upon the earth.' So God created humankind in his image, in the image of God he created them; male and female he created them (Gen 1:26-27).

In the story of creation in Genesis, human beings are the *only* creatures described as being like God. The Creator is, of course, present and is revealed in the whole of creation. We human beings, however, are like God in a *different* way; we are the only beings on earth who can seek and discover the truth, who can love, giving ourselves by our free choice to one another in compassionate and generous relationships. We can search and explore the depth of the mystery around us and within us; we can try to understand it and to express its meaning in science and art and music and literature and in how we live. That search is never over: it points towards a truth that we can never fully grasp. In all of that, we see a fundamental reason why human life is an image of God. We have in ourselves the ability to know and to choose and to love. We are rational and free. We discover truth, we express truth and we share it. Underlying all of that is a restless search for happiness and beauty and truth and goodness which have their source in God. Saint John Paul put it like this: 'objectively speaking, the search for truth and the search for God are one and the same'.[3]

Does life have a meaning?

The search for meaning can be frightening. The most terrifying fear is that it might lead nowhere, to mere emptiness, to the conclusion that life is absurd. That disturbing fear is impossible to avoid. Even a saint like Thérèse of Lisieux, who is often wrongly thought of as possessing a simplistic, even childish, faith, wrote:

> [God] allowed my soul to be overwhelmed with darkness, and the thought of Heaven, which had consoled me from

my earliest childhood, now became a subject of conflict and torture … I have been suffering for months, and I still await deliverance … One must have passed through this dark tunnel to understand its blackness … When I sing of the happiness of Heaven and the eternal possession of God, I do not feel any joy therein, for I sing only of what I wish to believe. Sometimes, I confess, a little ray of sunshine illumines my dark night, and I enjoy peace for an instant, but later, the remembrance of this ray of light, instead of consoling me, makes the blackness thicker still.[4]

Saint John Paul's encyclical on Faith and Reason said:

The truth comes initially to the human being as a question: *Does life have a meaning? Where is it going?* At first sight, personal existence may seem completely meaningless … The daily experience of suffering – in one's own life and in the lives of others – and the array of facts which seem inexplicable … are enough to ensure that a question as dramatic as the question of meaning cannot be evaded. Moreover, the first absolutely certain truth of our life, beyond the fact that we exist, is the inevitability of our death. Given this unsettling fact, the search for a full answer is inescapable … We want to know if death will be the definitive end of our life or if there is something beyond – if it is possible to hope for an after-life or not.[5]

To ask whether life may be meaningless is so disquieting a question that we may attempt to push it aside, or take refuge in short cuts that could never satisfy our longing. If we do not face the disturbing question, we cannot appreciate the wonder and amazement at ourselves which is called the Gospel.

We look into the sky at the tiny fraction of the universe that we can see. If we stop to reflect, we may allow ourselves to be humbled by the realisation that we live on a small planet, circling an insignificant star, in the outer part of the relatively small galaxy we call the Milky Way. The Milky Way contains at the lowest estimate, one hundred billion stars, many of them far larger than our sun. Our galaxy is one among one hundred billion to two hundred billion galaxies in the *visible* universe. As the Americans say 'do the math!' We are far from being at the centre of the universe!

By reflecting on all of that we can begin to glimpse the immensity of what it means to believe in the loving Creator, 'maker of heaven and earth, of all things visible and invisible.'[6] Only in Christ, the Incarnate Word of God, the image of the unseen God (Col 1:15), do we find the meaning that can satisfy us. His life, his death and his entry into a new creation, opens up the vision of an existence that fulfils all the deepest human hopes.

The great temptation is to settle for something less. All the wonderful things that attract us and fascinate us and challenge us can themselves become a replacement for ultimate meaning, and so become an obstacle to our growth into the likeness of God who is the source of *all* love, beauty, truth and joy.

Instead of seeing the beauty of the world as a reflection of God, instead of seeing our discoveries and our achievements and our creativity as signs that we are made in the image of God, we can reduce the truth to something on a human scale. We begin to think of our search as aiming at nothing more than a goal we imagine and seek to create for ourselves. That goal might be a scientific project or a political objective or a particular ambition or even a deep personal relationship. It may be very admirable in itself, but *it cannot be the meaning of life*. Even our closest relationships are vulnerable to death; even the greatest achievements crumble. Even what Genesis sees as the highest expression of human dignity, namely that we are made according to God's image and likeness, can become the ultimate temptation:

> The serpent said to the woman, 'You will not die; for God knows that when you eat of it your eyes will be opened, *and you will be like God*, knowing good and evil.' (Gen 3:4–5)

Thinking oneself to be 'like God' in that sense, is the most basic temptation. We begin to imagine that we can, so to speak, replace God; that we can be self-sufficient like God, and thus fail to recognise the source of our hope. But the goal we imagine for ourselves can never be big enough to satisfy us forever and in every aspect of our lives. If we regard even the greatest realities in creation as the answer to every human longing, they can obscure the truth. If they lead us to say, 'I need look no further', they deceive us. If we live for something less than God, we close our hearts and minds to the goal implicit in the world that God creates and sustains; we miss the limitless promise that God's invitation has written in our hearts.

If the goal we seek is to be one that is capable of fully satisfying us it must lie beyond imperfect and impermanent realities. The first act of hope, and of faith, is to believe that life is not absurd, and that, therefore, there is a hope big enough to satisfy our restless hearts.

Image and likeness

We say we are made in the image of God, but an image is only a statue or a painting, something that reminds us of the person who is represented. However good the likeness, it is merely a replica of the person it depicts. It may be a masterpiece, but it remains only an image. We are images of God, but 'We are not God'.[7] Perhaps the point can be more clearly seen if we return to the original text: God says 'Let us create humanity in our image,[8] according to our likeness'.[9] Those two words are often taken to mean much the same thing. But that is not the case, as is clear, especially in the Eastern Christian tradition. One Eastern Orthodox author writes:

> The expression 'according to the image', wrote John of Damascus, indicates rationality and freedom, while

the expression 'according to the likeness' indicates assimilation to God through virtue.[10]

There are two aspects to what Genesis tells us. We are made in the image of God, rational and free, capable of seeking the truth, capable of relating and loving. But being made in the image of God is not a static reality; it is also a task.

It means being called to use the gifts we have been given so as to play our part in God's love and care and responsibility for the whole of creation. By doing that, believing in the gift of God's love for us and seeking to receive it and *live* it, we grow into God's likeness and into recognition of one another, 'welcoming the entire world as a gift from the Father and our common home'.[11]

The *image* of God is found above all in the fact that the human person is rational and free. *Likeness* to God, on the other hand, is a growing participation in God's life, a participation which begins in a particularly explicit way through Baptism. God's image and likeness, of course, are not confined to those who are baptised. As Vatican II put it, since Christ died for all, 'we ought to believe that the Holy Spirit in a manner known only to God offers to everyone the possibility of being associated with this paschal mystery'.[12]

Likeness grows through our cooperation with God, though it remains always God's free gift. Our efforts are *efforts to accept* what God freely offers us, not attempts to grasp it for ourselves and take possession of it, still less to create it for ourselves. Grasping is the opposite of receiving a gift. We receive a gift with open hands, we grasp something with our hands firmly locked around it. This is a crucial point. Being in the likeness of God grows through our co-operation with what is and always remains God's gift. We cannot really cooperate with it unless we recognise that it is a *gift*.

Only the infinite can fill the heart

Every human achievement is imperfect and fragile. Even the greatest of them cannot provide meaning to every human life in every time and place and culture. Even the best plans can fail, even the most wonderful people die – and often they die young. Nothing we can do could repair the injustice done to generations of people who have died in poverty, slavery or oppression. We cannot help those who have died except by praying to God for them. Only God can reach them.

It is good that we should have all sorts of goals and projects, but we need what Pope Benedict called the great hope which can only be God.[13] The truth is, he said, 'that finite things can give glimpses of joy, but *only the Infinite can fill the heart*'.[14] We are dependent on God for a hope big enough to embrace all the suffering of every human life throughout history, a hope big enough to satisfy all the longings of every human heart. No human effort could do that.

Saint Irenaeus, writing about AD 180, is often quoted as saying that 'the glory of God is man (humanity) fully alive'. That version is slightly inaccurate and it is incomplete.[15] The text is better translated as, 'The glory of God is the living human being;

and the life of the human being consists in beholding God'. And it goes on to say: '... if the manifestation of God which is made by means of the creation, affords life to all living in the earth, much more does that revelation of the Father which comes through the Word, give life to those who see God.'[16] Irenaeus is saying that the glory of God is not so much the great fullness of life and joy that people can experience from time to time, but the fact that we exist as beings who are capable of knowing, loving and therefore reflecting God. He goes on to say that the purpose of our existence is to know the God who made us during our lives on earth and so arrive, after our death, at the fullest sharing in that life, beholding God face to face.

The misquotation, says something important, but only if one interprets the phrase 'fully alive' according to the context Irenaeus gives it. After all, people may say that a full life, or at least a less empty life, is what they are seeking in the abuse of drugs, in promiscuity, in having their own way in everything. To say that human life is about beholding God means that its meaning is to be found deeper than our immediate wants and needs, achievements and experiences, and far beyond them, in a relationship with the Creator.

The challenge of being human

That is the challenge of living so as to grow into the likeness of God who is love. Too often a life of faith is seen to consist in obeying rules or believing a series of statements. These things have their place, but the heart of the challenge is not about keeping rules or about knowing facts, not even about studying theology. Neither is the meaning of life to be found in being wealthy or popular or influential.

Pope Benedict XVI devoted his life to the study of theology. He was particularly concerned about the disintegration of fundamental moral values, what he called 'the dictatorship of relativism'. When he preached at the Mass which began the conclave that was to elect him as Pope he listed that as a great challenge facing the Church.[17] Yet when he described the essential meaning of Christianity in the opening section of his first encyclical, he explicitly said that these two things, important as they are, are not where the centre of Christian life is to be found:

> Being Christian is not the result of an ethical choice or a lofty idea, but the encounter with an event, a person, which gives life a new horizon and a decisive direction.[18]

In the opening words of that encyclical, he points to St John's summary of the Christian life: '*We have come to know and to believe in the love God has for us.*'[19]

He made the same point just before he became Pope at the funeral of Fr Luigi Giussani, the founder of Communion and Liberation:

> [Fr Giussani] ... understood that Christianity is not an intellectual system, a packet of dogmas, a moralism, Christianity is rather an encounter, a love story; it is an

event. This love affair with Christ, this love story that was the whole of Giussani's life, was at the same time quite far removed from any superficial enthusiasm or vague romanticism. Seeing Christ, Giussani truly knew that to encounter Christ means to follow him.[20]

So the core of it is not about moral principles or theological ideas, still less about achievements, status or possessions; it is about an encounter, a relationship, with God, particularly through 'a love affair with Christ'. If, as Irenaeus said, the living human being makes the glory of God visible, that is true in a supreme way in Jesus Christ. He is the human being who perfectly reveals God; he is God's perfect image and his perfect likeness: 'Whoever has seen me has seen the Father' (Jn 14:9). Paul speaks of how Jesus is the fulfilment of the image and likeness of God in humankind:

> [God] has rescued us from the power of darkness and transferred us into the kingdom of his beloved Son, in whom we have redemption, the forgiveness of sins. He is the image of the invisible God, the firstborn of all creation; for in him all things in heaven and on earth were created, things visible and invisible, whether thrones or dominions or rulers or powers – all things have been created through him and for him … He himself is before all things, and in him all things hold together. (Col 1:13-17)

In Second Corinthians, Paul talks about how the image of God, the truth of the Good News, can become obscured, but, he adds, Jesus who is *the* image of God 'has shone in our hearts to give the light of the knowledge of the glory of God in the face of Jesus Christ' (2 Cor 4: 4-6).

For those who follow Jesus, growing into the likeness of God means recognising God's perfect likeness in the life, death and resurrection of his Son. It means recognising that we depend on the generous gift of God, who sent his only Son so that we might have life in him (Jn 3:16). We depend on God, who is love, for our very existence and for the possibility of growing into what God's free gift has made us capable of becoming. The ultimate temptation is to exert influence over others, or our own image of ourselves, or getting our own way, or *anything other than God*, the goal of our lives. The temptation is to turn our back on that gift and thus to deny what is deepest in ourselves.

We are not alone

Saint John Paul wrote of the wonder and amazement of seeing ourselves in the light of Christ who has shone in our hearts.[21] We will not grasp the depth of that amazement *simply* by reflecting on ourselves. At an ecumenical meeting some years ago some of us proposed that we might look at the question: 'who are we?' – in other words that we would reflect on the topic of Christian anthropology. The Orthodox representatives willingly cooperated in the project, but they regarded our western approach as too individualistic. We cannot grasp the

Christian, or even, the human, vision of who we are unless we begin by seeing that being 'a person' is essentially about being in relationship, with God, with one another and with the world.

In *Laudato Si'* Pope Francis speaks about the relationships which are central to understanding ourselves:

> [The creation accounts in Genesis] suggest that human life is grounded in three fundamental and closely intertwined relationships: with *God*, with our *neighbour* and with the *earth* itself. According to the Bible, these three vital relationships have been broken, both outwardly and within us. This rupture is sin. The harmony between the Creator, humanity and creation as a whole was disrupted by our presuming to take the place of God and refusing to acknowledge our creaturely limitations.[22]

We are in a series of relationships which are intertwined; and we might add to the three our relationship with ourselves.[23] We need to care for all of these relationships – with God, with others, with the world and with ourselves. Without taking all of these into account we cannot really understand who we are or what should guide our behaviour.

The Trinity and creation

The word 'person' has to do with relationships even when it is applied to God. Pope Francis says:

> The divine Persons are subsistent relations, and the world, created according to the divine model, is a web of relationships. Creatures tend towards God, and in turn it is proper to every living being to tend towards other things, so that throughout the universe we can find any number of constant and secretly interwoven relationships.[24]

The interconnectedness, or 'entanglement', seems to show itself in ways we hardly begin to understand. There appears to be a phenomenon in quantum physics where what happens in one system is reflected in another instantaneously, even at great distances.[25] This action over vast distances is also a feature of the recently confirmed 'gravitational waves' predicted by Einstein.[26] Whatever about such as yet poorly understood connectedness in quantum physics and mechanics – I speak not least for myself – everything that exists is immediately, permanently and intimately connected with the Creator who brought it into existence and who sustains it in existence.

At the foundation of any growth in holiness is the realisation that my relationship with God is a relationship with the One to whom everything in this universe is related and on whom everything is dependent. I cannot relate to God as if only God and I existed. Each of our relationships with God is part of the 'web of relationships' which is the created universe. And that web of relationships goes to the heart of the divine creativity. It shows that our universe is created by the unimaginable flow of the divine life, a flow of goodness, truth, beauty and unity infinitely beyond any experience we have of those qualities:

> The Father is the ultimate source of everything, the loving and self-communicating foundation of all that exists. The Son, his reflection, through whom all things were created, united himself to this earth when he was formed in the womb of Mary. The Spirit, infinite bond of love, is intimately present at the very heart of the universe, inspiring and bringing new pathways. The world was created by the three Persons acting as a single divine principle, but each one of them performed this common work in accordance with his own personal property. Consequently, 'when we contemplate with wonder the universe in all its grandeur and beauty, we must praise the whole Trinity'.[27]

The key to our fulfilment

This, Pope Francis says, is 'the key to our own fulfilment' and he goes on to say:

> The human person grows more, matures more and is sanctified more to the extent that he or she enters into relationships, going out from themselves to live in communion with God, with others and with all creatures. In this way, they make their own that Trinitarian dynamism which God imprinted in them when they were

created. Everything is interconnected, and this invites us to develop a spirituality of that global solidarity which flows from the mystery of the Trinity.[28]

The key lies in the relationships identified in the encyclical and celebrated in the Eucharist.

Our relationship with the earth: Gerard Manley Hopkins wrote, 'The world is charged with the grandeur of God'.[29] Our relationship with the world is part of how we relate to the Creator. Pope Francis in *Laudato Si'* quotes St Bonaventure: 'contemplation deepens the more we feel the working of God's grace within our hearts, and the better we learn to encounter God in creatures outside ourselves'.[30]

In celebrating the Eucharist, we gather up all the ways in which God's creatures – in the animal and plant and inanimate world – wordlessly praise his glory. In our lives and our prayers, and above all in the Eucharist, we give voice to that praise in what St John Paul referred to as humanity's role as the spokespersons for all creation.[31]

Our relationship with others: In the Eucharist we celebrate the summit of the life of the Church. We are in the presence of the fulfilment of the Church's *raison d'être*: to be 'a sign and instrument both of a very closely knit union with God and of the unity of the whole human race'.[32] We gather around the Risen Lord who is drawing all people to himself.[33]

At the same time, there would be a deep contradiction between expressing our hope to be part of God's people gathered in the eternal house of our Father while being alienated from some of the very people God has invited to that gathering in which all will be made new. We ought always to feel the need to be reconciled with our brothers and sisters before coming to offer the gift of ourselves with Christ to the Father (cf. Mt 5:24).

In our sharing in the Eucharist we should feel the gigantic remorse that should follow from the contrast between great wealth and horrific famine and hardship in the world.[34] Many of us, Pope Francis points out, 'live and reason from the comfortable position of a high level of development and a quality of life well beyond the reach of the majority of the world's population'.[35]

Our relationship with ourselves: Participating in the celebration of the Eucharist also raises the challenge of our relationship with ourselves. In particular, the very notion of the Sabbath rest and Sabbath celebration points to the need to try constantly to see ourselves and our lives in greater depth. We gather for Sunday Mass to recognise who we really are and where our lives lead. We gather to celebrate what we call 'the meaning of life'. It is extraordinary how that most fundamental question can seem so unreal and impractical in the midst of what we imagine are 'the important issues' of life. The Eucharist is the summit and source of our lives.[36] It challenges us to reflect with the Christian community on who we are. We do that in Eucharist, in the context of the great act of Christian thanksgiving. The real meaning of our lives is to receive with never-ending gratitude, God's gift which touches us in deep in our hearts. Pope Francis wrote in *Laudato Si'*:

> It is in the Eucharist that all that has been created finds its greatest exaltation ... The Lord, in the culmination of the mystery of the Incarnation, chose to reach our intimate depths through a fragment of matter. He comes not from above, but from within, he comes that we might find him in this world of ours. In the Eucharist, fullness is already achieved; it is the living centre of the universe, the overflowing core of love and of inexhaustible life. Joined to the incarnate Son, present in the Eucharist, the whole cosmos gives thanks to God. Indeed, the Eucharist is itself an act of cosmic love.[37]

Chapter Two

A Meagre Awareness

People of all times and places have always had blind spots. One thinks of the failure of western cultures to see the evils of slavery until the nineteenth century and how this horrific injustice still exists today in the form of human trafficking. The most disconcerting aspect of recognising the blindness in past generations is that it challenges us to recognise our own blind spots. Pope Francis puts it starkly: 'Each age tends to have only a meagre awareness of its own limitations'.[1]

One of our blind spots is that contemporary culture reflects rarely, if at all, on the fundamentally mysterious aspect of ourselves. A mystery, as Gabriel Marcel describes it, is something that I cannot understand with objectivity 'from the outside', because I am part of it, and it is part of me.

> A problem is something which I meet, which I find complete before me ... But a mystery is something in which I myself am involved ... A genuine problem is subject to an appropriate technique by the exercise of

which it is defined; whereas a mystery, by definition, transcends every conceivable technique.[2]

Recognising our blind spots

We can never completely grasp the blind spots of our own time because that would require us fully to answer to the question, 'Who are we?' It would require us to be able to understand all the ways in which we interact with the world in which we live, all the ways we influence it, and all the ways in which it influences us.

Human culture is mysterious in an even more fundamental sense. Saint John Paul said:

> At the heart of every culture lies the attitude (the human being) takes to the greatest mystery: the mystery of God.

He goes on to express that truth in another way:

> Different cultures are basically different ways of facing the question of the meaning of personal existence. When this question is eliminated, the culture and moral life of nations are corrupted.[3]

Does *our* blind spot consist, perhaps, in a kind of emptiness that seems to lie at the heart of much of our culture? A stranger looking at the western world might conclude that our societies appear to have little concern for the meaning of personal existence. What Saint John Paul called, 'the great forces which shape the world – politics, the mass media, science, technology, culture, education, industry and work ...'[4] show little evidence that they are infused with an awareness of, still less guided by, the question at the heart of human life: 'the question of the meaning of personal existence', still less by the mystery of God. One might ask what is the inspiration and energy at the heart of our culture.

The people who come after us will, we hope, find things to be grateful for, things to admire, in our generation. They will also undoubtedly find reasons to look back at us, as we do at other generations, and say 'How could they have been so blind?' Perhaps the most fundamental of these reasons will be that they will see us as having possessed previously unimaginable means of changing the world, wielding immense power, great technological expertise and unprecedented global communications, while rarely thinking it relevant to ask what human life is for, what it means or where it leads.

There are, of course, people – artists, poets, philosophers, playwrights, contemplatives – who do ask fundamental questions. Nevertheless, life in modern Ireland, and in the Western world in general, appears to be guided, not by an overall vision of the meaning of personal existence, but, at best, by what Pope Benedict called 'lesser hopes'. These are particular goals and projects: economic growth, equity in society, and freedom from violence which are useful, even necessary, to our lives, but are not the meaning of our existence. None of them can provide an overriding goal for every aspect of life:

A distortion of our understanding of ourselves arises from the virtual silencing in our world of deep questions of meaning and of the mystery of a God of love who is our hope. Saint John Paul said that many people today are 'often unable to be silent for fear of meeting [themselves], of feeling the emptiness that asks itself about meaning'.[5] The emptiness arises because we are afraid of the truth about ourselves. The anxiety that life might have no meaning leads to emptiness and loss of coherence. Saint Francis of Assisi points us rather to the wonder that lies at what his namesake, Pope Francis, calls 'the heart of what it is to be human'.[6]

> His response to the world around him was so much more than intellectual appreciation or economic calculus, for to him each and every creature was a sister united to him by bonds of affection … If we approach nature and the environment without this openness to awe and wonder, if we no longer speak the language of fraternity and beauty in our relationship with the world, our attitude will be that of masters, consumers, ruthless exploiters, unable to set limits on their immediate needs. By contrast, if we feel intimately united with all that exists, then sobriety and care will well up spontaneously. The poverty and austerity of Saint Francis were no mere veneer of asceticism, but something much more radical: a refusal to turn reality into an object simply to be used and controlled.[7]

A 'great emptiness' reflects itself in many areas of life, and in a particular way in the area of moral reasoning.

Filling the emptiness

We ask ourselves what all of this means for Christians and the Christian understanding of human life. We also need to ask whether Christians have anything to say to our brothers and sisters who do not believe in Christ, or in God, but who are equally entitled to play their part in the life of society? All the world views, philosophies and religions existing in society have a legitimate role in the discussion of public policy. Healthy pluralism can, however, be undermined in various ways, some of them subtle and scarcely noticed. For instance, it sometimes seems that atheistic and humanist views are presumed to be completely neutral and entirely rational, whereas Christian or other religious belief is seen simply as 'an opinion' without any rational foundation or any right to be considered. While it is often said that the latter views 'should be respected', this respect sometimes amounts to very little in practice. That is not surprising if one starts from the premise that these views are irrational, or at least that they are irrelevant in public discourse.

It is also true, and the consequences continue to be seen and heard, that in the Catholic culture of Ireland in the past, as in many overwhelmingly uniform cultures, many people had reason to feel overwhelmed or unheard. But a failure to hear and respect alternative views in the past, provides a lesson to be learned, not an example to be followed.

The way in which we all come to know moral values and obligations is through the human heart. That should not simply mean 'whatever attracts me at the moment'. Our heart means the deepest place within us, the place where we are alone with God.[8]

Christian morality does not seek to propose answers which are in conflict with the truth of who we are. Nor does the Catholic Church seek to use the law of the state to coerce people into accepting its moral and social teaching:

> The Church's social teaching argues on the basis of reason and natural law, namely, on the basis of what is in accord with the nature of every human being. It recognises that it is not the Church's responsibility to make this teaching prevail. Rather, the Church wishes to help form consciences in political life and to stimulate greater insight into the authentic requirements of justice as well as greater readiness to act accordingly, even when this might involve conflict with situations of personal interest.[9]

The Law of Christ

Saint Thomas Aquinas did not see the New Law of Christ as imposing obligations which did not already arise from our understanding of our own dignity. The obligations arising from the respect due to human dignity are already expressed in the Ten Commandments. Accordingly,

> ... the New Law had no other external works to determine, by prescribing or forbidding, except the sacraments, and those moral precepts which have a necessary connection with virtue ...[10]

This New Law is not primarily about rules. Christian moral teaching is not to be found principally in the Ten Commandments.

> The Commandments properly so-called come in the second place: they express the implications of belonging to God through the establishment of the covenant. Moral existence is a response to the Lord's loving initiative.[11]

This Lord's loving initiative, expressed in the covenant with the Jewish people, reaches out, as we have seen, to every human being. That primal invitation is what gives all human beings a dignity that we cannot give ourselves and a hope, beyond what we can see, hear or conceive, the only hope that can fully satisfy the aspirations of our hearts.[12]

The Law of Christ, therefore, is not about adding to the rules, rather it adds a depth and intensity to our obligation to be just, compassionate, faithful and truthful. These virtues are about responding to what is best in our own humanity, rather than to obligations imposed from outside.

Precisely because of this 'truth' the natural law involves universality. Inasmuch as it is inscribed in the rational nature of the person, it makes itself felt to all beings endowed with reason and living in history. In order to perfect a person in his/her specific order, the person must do good and avoid evil, be concerned for the transmission and preservation of life, refine and develop the riches of the material world, cultivate social life, seek truth, practise good and contemplate beauty.[13]

So what is distinctive about what Christian faith contributes to society?

The encyclical *Veritatis Splendor* begins with the question of the rich young man: 'What must I do to inherit eternal life?' For Saint John Paul this was fundamental:

In the young man, whom Matthew's Gospel does not name, we can recognise every person who, consciously or not, *approaches Christ the Redeemer of man and questions him about morality*. For the young man, the question is not so much about rules to be followed, but *about the full meaning of life*. This is in fact the aspiration at the heart of every human decision and action, the quiet searching and interior prompting which sets freedom in motion. This question is ultimately an appeal to the absolute Good which attracts us and beckons us; it is the echo of a call from God who is the origin and goal of man's life.[14]

Although Jesus points the rich young man to the commandments, he moves him on to see that more is at stake than obedience to rules – true and binding though these fundamental rules are. Such rules cannot simply dictate political and social solutions for widely different times and contexts. They point rather to the dignity and meaning of human life and, in particular, to the fundamental nature of human morality.

But religious belief has an essential contribution to the good of society. Pope Benedict pointed to two ways in which faith enriches understanding:

> Faith is a purifying force for reason … it liberates reason from its blind spots and therefore helps it to be ever more fully itself …[15]
>
> [The Church] has to play her part through rational argument and she has to reawaken the spiritual energy without which justice, which always demands sacrifice, cannot prevail and prosper.[16]

Christian faith does not provide solutions to moral questions which differ from what justice and love demand, nor does it seek to impose irrational solutions. Faith sees all of this as part of the 'only response fully capable of satisfying the desire of the human heart'. On the other hand, to say that moral and social questions have nothing to do with faith or with the churches, would, in effect, do two things. It would imply that there is no ultimate truth, no 'lofty vocation' underlying our choices. The

Gospel as we saw, does not point to moral, political or social conclusions different from those sought by human reason. The faith of the Church, that is of the whole Christian community, certainly not exclusively of the hierarchy,[17] contributes to the conscientious search for truth in which 'Christians are joined to others'.[18] Faith is relevant also because it challenges a narrowness of perspective and the temptation to treat some other people as less than the brothers and sisters with whom we are called to share eternal solidarity and joy. Faith gives us the example of Christians down the centuries who sought to love, as Jesus did, even to giving their lives for others.

Secondly, to regard faith as irrelevant is to fail to see the role of fundamental convictions, including convictions not expressed in religious terms, in providing the spiritual energy society needs. Any choice we make is an expression, however distorted, of our fundamental drive for the fulfilment that can satisfy us; in religious terms it is a longing for what God has prepared for us. The rich young man knew that, but our society lives in many respects 'as though God does not exist'. God has for many disappeared below people's existential horizon.[19] In a society, where fundamental issues of meaning have no place, the level of discussion and reflection on political, social and moral issues is likely to be shallow. One might think that the level of political discussion in Western societies provides countless examples of this shallowness. Faith challenges us to see others, however different or distant as people in whose name Jesus will say: 'I was hungry or thirsty or sick or in prison, and you did or did not come to my aid'. It reminds us that we live in a world in which people suffer intolerable injustice. Faith shows us that every time we make a choice we are responding in some way to the longing within us, which comes from God's invitation, for our ultimate fulfilment and that of the entire human family.

Chapter Three

Redrawing the Landscape

Nowhere in modern society is the inadequacy of reflection on these fundamental questions as clear as in the area of moral thinking. The moral consensus in Western society has altered dramatically in recent times with little serious reflection on why this has happened or whether it is a good thing. Jonathan Sacks, the former Chief Rabbi in Britain, described the transformation:

> To make moral judgements is to be judgemental. Calling a way of life wrong is an assault on the integrity or authenticity of others. The most fundamental of all parental wishes, to educate our children in our own morality, is indoctrination and a denial of their free development.[1]

He refers to the implications of this change:

> The gradual transformation by which sin becomes immorality, immorality becomes deviance, deviance becomes choice and all choice becomes legitimate, is *a profound redrawing of our moral landscape*.[2]

The widespread acceptance of abortion on request in many parts of our world would have been unthinkable, even to those judges and politicians in various countries who facilitated what they claimed, and presumably believed, would be strictly limited abortion. What we tend to see is many debates about deeply felt issues that can hardly be called debate in the proper sense. The opposing viewpoints do not engage with one another. There often seems to be scarcely any meeting of minds, but rather mutual incomprehension.

It would hardly be convincing to claim that this transformation is the result of sudden widespread enlightenment about an unforeseen, but now obvious, truth unimagined by previous generations. Some reflection will show that the redrawing of our landscape is by no means inexplicable, but follows from the increasing predominance of a different approach to evaluating our moral decisions. There has been little discussion, or even awareness, of the foundations and weaknesses of that approach,

Utilitarian moral philosophy was formulated in the nineteenth century as an attempt to give moral thinking a solid base in the context of the new scientific world view and of the scientific method.[3] Some would trace its origins back to Greek philosophers like Epicurus. It is important to understand something about this philosophy because it underlies almost every moral debate in the new landscape.

In coming to a decision, the Utilitarian asks one basic question: will our choice produce more happiness or pleasure than pain or distress? Or, to put it another way, will it add to the sum of human happiness? This approach has come to be seen by many as unproblematic and even self-evident.

The problems that this implies have often been expressed. The early Utilitarians spoke about a 'calculus' as a way of measuring the pleasure and pain that would be produced by an action. This sounds like a scientific term but in the moral context such a 'calculation' cannot provide scientific accuracy. Happiness and pain cannot be mathematically calculated because enjoyment or distress, happiness or pleasure, even in very similar circumstances, may vary from person to person and even in the same person from time to time. There is no way of 'calculating' the value of different kinds of pleasure – listening to music, being with friends – nor of comparing different kinds of pain or distress – hunger, loneliness or guilt. The idea that moral decision making could be a kind of scientific process based on measuring pleasure and pain is ultimately an illusion. Such an approach ignores a vital point made by Aristotle at the beginning of his *Nicomachean Ethics,* namely that it is the mark of the educated person 'to look for precision in each class of things just so far as the nature of the subject admits'.[4]

Ironically, in view of the argumentation used in many aspects of the document, the report on IVF and related matters chaired by Dame Mary Warnock began by pointing out the weakness of the utilitarian approach:

> A strict utilitarian would suppose that, given certain procedures, it would be possible to calculate their

> benefits and their costs. Future advantages, therapeutic or scientific, should be weighed against present and future harm. However, even if such a calculation were possible, it could not provide a final or verifiable answer to the question whether it is right that such procedures should be carried out. There would still remain the possibility that they were unacceptable, whatever their longterm benefits were supposed to be. Moral questions, such as those with which we have been concerned are, by definition, questions that involve not only a calculation of consequences, but also strong sentiments with regard to the nature of the proposed activities themselves.[5]

One would have to question the reduction of what are basic moral principles to the status of 'strong sentiments', but the question of whether such calculations are really possible and the recognition that they cannot answer the question whether an action is right or wrong, neatly sums up the weakness of Utilitarianism.

Teasing out the question

What is said above is of great importance even if it seems to complicate the question; but it would be unfortunate, in a democracy where everybody has a responsibility for the decisions and policies that are adopted, if people were tempted to think that some issues and some discussions are 'beyond them'. It would be a great pity if arguments, crucial to the outcome, were dismissed as rarefied, abstract or complicated.

It is *essential* for the health of our societies that we find ways of addressing the mutual incomprehension between different approaches to morality. There will be many more debates in the years ahead. If these issues are not addressed, the redrawing of the moral landscape will continue without any serious examination of the foundations on which the decisions being taken by our society are based.

The problem of competing moral languages is precisely the question addressed by one of Saint John Paul's most important encyclicals, *Veritatis Splendor*. Commenting on its importance, Pope Benedict outlined how, at the time of Vatican II, and particularly in the writing of *Gaudium et Spes*, the Council Fathers felt that arguments from natural law (that is arguing on the basis of the truth of 'who we are'), were losing their impact and they sought instead to build morality on the basis of the Christian vision of life. That project was only partially successful because the apparent contrast of the two approaches cannot be sustained. The Christian vision is also about who we are.[6] This left a vacuum which St John Paul set out to fill in *Veritatis Splendor*. Pope Benedict concluded that 'the great task that John Paul II took on in this encyclical was that of rediscovering a metaphysical foundation in anthropology, as also a Christian concretisation in the new image of the human being in Sacred Scripture. *Studying and assimilating this encyclical remains a great and important duty*'.[7] In other words we need a deeper understanding of who we are, of what it means to be human (anthropology) and a better appreciation of the light that Christian faith sheds on how we understand ourselves.

The great task

A great deal of that widespread study and assimilation of *Veritatis Splendor* still remains to be done. As a result, we are being swamped, without appreciating the significance of what is happening, by a Utilitarian language of moral discussion which, as the encyclical shows, is incapable of taking account of the richness of the Christian moral vision and which does not reflect an adequate concept of human dignity.

Utilitarianism undermines the understanding of human dignity on which Christian morality is founded: the deep wonder and amazement at human worth and dignity which St John Paul said, 'is the Gospel', and 'is also called Christianity'.[8] That is not at all to suggest that undermining Christian morality is the intention of those who approach moral thinking in this way. But the overwhelming assumption that moral discussion must be Utilitarian, gives little ground for hoping that we will have a society in which rational discussion which recognises that Catholic morality is founded on a profound understanding of human dignity will be possible – even among Catholics!

The new landscape brings concerns about the implications for freedom of conscientious expression and action in some social, political, medical and educational decisions. There needs to be space in parliament, in hospitals, in schools and in daily life for expressing one's mind freely, for questioning the consensus. This is enormously important for a healthy society. The integrity of politics and respect for politicians is not enhanced if those who have been elected to represent the people are clearly uncomfortable with the way they feel obliged to vote in carrying out their role.

Veritatis Splendor analyses what the Utilitarian approach does to a Christian understanding of human life and human freedom. A number of things emerge from this.

Human freedom

The response of many people to socially controversial issues will be informed by a desire to show concern and to bring happiness to people who feel disadvantaged in society. *Veritatis Splendor* shows, however, that to see this as the *only* issue oversimplifies what moral decision making involves. There are many dimensions – including, of course, seeking to counter suffering, disadvantage and exclusion – that need to be taken into account if we are to do justice to human dignity and freedom. Some important dimensions are largely missing in contemporary discussion. The encyclical asks:

> … on what does the moral assessment of [a person's] free acts depend? What is it that ensures this ordering of human acts to God? Is it the intention of the acting subject, the circumstances – and in particular the consequences – of his action, or the object itself of his act?[9]

That is probably the most crucial point that the encyclical makes. We must of course consider the circumstances and consequences of our actions – failure to do so would be irresponsible; and we must also evaluate honestly the intentions that motivate our choices, since apparently good things can be done for corrupt or hypocritical reasons; however, the most fundamental question is this: 'what it is that we are choosing to do in attempting to achieve good results'? This, Pope John Paul calls 'the object itself of the person's act'.

Because it fails to see the importance of that question, as Lady Warnock concisely showed, Utilitarianism succumbs to an approach that is content to think that, 'the end justifies the means'. This is, in the proper sense of the word, 'irresponsible'; it does not take responsibility for what it is that I am choosing to do, claiming that this may be disregarded in the interests of achieving a desirable end result.

The encyclical makes a perceptive observation about the Utilitarian, consequentialist kinds of approach:

> These theories can gain a certain persuasive force from their affinity to the scientific mentality, which is rightly concerned with ordering technical and economic activities on the basis of a calculation of resources and profits, procedures and their effects. They seek to provide liberation from the constraints of a voluntaristic and arbitrary morality of obligation which would ultimately be dehumanising. Such theories however are not faithful to

the Church's teaching, when they believe they can justify, as morally good, deliberate choices of kinds of behaviour contrary to the commandments of the divine and natural law. These theories cannot claim to be grounded in the Catholic moral tradition.[10]

What do we choose?

It is not enough to point to the wonderful consequences or to my high motives if what I have chosen to do is simply wrong – a violation of my own dignity and that of others, a denial of the truth about myself and the people my choice affects. *Veritatis Splendor* speaks of what it is that we choose to do as 'the object'. If the object is wrong, then no good intention or no good consequence can make the choice morally right. It follows that there are some kinds of choice which can never be justified:

> Reason attests that there are objects of the human act which are by their nature 'incapable of being ordered' to God, because they radically contradict the good of the person made in his image. These are the acts which, in the Church's moral tradition, have been termed 'intrinsically evil' (*intrinsece malum*):[11] they are such always and *per se*, in other words, on account of their very object, and quite apart from the ulterior intentions of the one acting and the circumstances. Consequently, without in the least denying the influence on morality exercised by circumstances and especially by intentions, the Church teaches that 'there

exist acts which *per se* and in themselves, independently of circumstances, are always seriously wrong by reason of their object'.[12]

Examples of such an act would be genocide, slavery, the deliberate killing of an innocent person, the use of torture, the abuse of a child, or anything which destroys human life and dignity.[13] It is important to understand that the 'object' is not simply an event, an objective occurrence. It is a deliberate choice:

> The object of the act of willing is in fact a freely chosen kind of behaviour.[14]

What we choose to do is not simply a physical occurrence in the world around us. Some natural disasters or accidents produce results which destroy human lives or cause great suffering, but 'a freely chosen kind of behaviour' is not a mere event; it can be properly understood only when it is seen in the light of that free choice.[15]

In every choice, especially the more significant ones, there are several dimensions:

> It has been rightly pointed out that freedom is not only the choice for one or another particular action; it is also, within that choice, a decision about oneself and a setting of one's own life for or against the Good, for or against the Truth, and ultimately for or against God.[16]

When a person is described as generous or truthful, or untrustworthy, or arrogant, these statements, however unkind some of them may be, are based on how the person consistently behaves. We realise that our choices are choices about the kind of people we will become. They are also choices about how we regard or disregard others. They are ultimately choices about the goal of our lives. What I choose to do contributes to making me a particular kind of person.

Freedom and nature

The temptation by the serpent in the Garden of Eden says something very relevant to our time. 'If you eat of the fruit of the tree, you will be like gods, knowing good and evil'. This is the temptation to see humanity as having complete control over nature, to decide what things will mean, to mould nature to our own 'needs' without any reference to the meaning given to human life by God, a meaning that is the answer to the question, 'who am I?' One aspect of the cultural revolution has been to deny that there is any 'given reality'. It often seems to see children, for instance, as entirely blank canvasses, or perhaps, blank computer discs, which can be programmed in a whole new way according to the latest views about what society needs and what we want its future to be. The looming ecological disaster is one symptom of such an attitude.

Our world tempts us to see our own nature and our world as an obstacle to our freedom and as infinitely manipulable. Pope Francis says we have forgotten that a human being 'is not only a freedom which he creates for himself. Man [the human being] does not create him or herself. He is spirit and will, but also nature'.[17] An attempt to create oneself is doomed to failure.

> [A Christian] knows that he harms himself and damages his environment when he denies natural laws, uses things in ways contrary to their intrinsic order, and tries to be wiser than God who created them. It demands too much of a person when he tries to design himself from start to finish.[18]

All of this suggests that what is at stake is not just a matter of moral theories. It is more fundamentally about the nature of humanity and in particular, the nature of human freedom.

Cultural shift or cultural suicide?

We are reluctant to consider apocalyptic visions. But we are facing a huge and unpredictable cultural, political, moral and ecological shift. Desmond Fennell wrote an essay, 'Ireland after the End of Western Civilisation', in which he said that the cultural experiments by which the West moved away from its roots: Communism, Nazism/Fascism and Liberal Capitalism, have all failed. He wrote:

> Those three efforts viewed together, each of them supported by millions of people, indicated a strong conviction among twentieth century Europeans, in Europe

and overseas, that the civilisation which their ancestors created, and which had enabled them to dominate and lead the world, had ended its usefulness – had had its day ...

The period since then, and continuing ahead of us beyond the collapse of the American liberal utopia, future historians will call 'transitional' and compare it to the transitional period between the civilisations of ancient Rome and Europe ... It will end in a new civilisation, or civilisations, in the West.[19]

He was not predicting anarchy, but rather the emergence of something new and unpredictable, which will be very different from what we have known as western civilisation – possibly better, but perhaps a great deal worse.

Nor should we ignore the statements of Pope Francis which are indeed apocalyptic. He views with great urgency the challenge that has been presented to us by Vatican II, and by his predecessors. The Council warned over fifty years ago that 'Our age more than any of the past needs ... wisdom ... Indeed the future of the world is in danger unless wiser people are forthcoming'.[20]

Pope Francis has spoken strongly about crucial nature of the challenge. In *Laudato Si'*, he quotes Pope Benedict writing in *Veritas in Caritate* about: 'the excitement and drama of human history, in which freedom, growth, salvation and love can blossom, or lead towards decadence and mutual destruction.

The work of the Church seeks not only to remind everyone of the duty to care for nature, but at the same time 'she must above all protect mankind from self-destruction'.[21] He quotes Paul VI speaking to the United Nations about the potential for an 'ecological catastrophe under the effective explosion of industrial civilisation'.[22]

In this context one might note several references in *Laudato Si'* to Romano Guardini's book, *The End of the Modern World*.[23] The book gathers a series of lectures given in the late 1940s. In his introduction to the 1998 edition, Richard Neuhaus sums up Guardini's thesis with a phrase attributed to Robert Jenson, 'the world has lost its story'.[24] The old stories are gone, he says; the life of faith will be lonely, but courage can base itself on the love revealed in Christ. That love means that hope always remains. Might we perhaps, he asks, come to 'experience this love anew, to taste the sovereignty of its origin, to know its independence of the world, to sense the mystery of its final why?'[25]

Even apart from ecological threats, Pope Francis has several times presented a bleak picture of the level of political and social threats. Most striking, perhaps, are his references to *Lord of the World*, a book written by Robert Hugh Benson in 1907. It tells of a world divided into hostile regions – the East, Europe and America. Religion, in particular Catholicism, is barely tolerated. A charismatic figure arises who promises world peace; vast numbers flock to acclaim him as the saviour. A new 'religion' without God is established and increasing pressure is put on Catholics to join this new world order. Gradually this becomes full scale persecution. Finally, the military forces of the new order descend on the last remnants of Catholicism gathered in Nazareth, determined to destroy them. As the last Pope celebrates Benediction, and as what seems to be the inevitable final annihilation of the Church draws closer, the book ends with the chilling words: 'Then this world passed and the glory of it'.

Pope Francis describes the book as prophetic 'almost as if the author could foresee what was going to happen'.[26] He has also indicated at least one aspect of what he sees as prophetic. It describes a world where one way of thinking becomes, in effect, compulsory. He has spoken several times about the danger of what he calls *'il pensiero unico'*[27] – the only [permitted] way of thinking.

Respect for the search for truth, in ourselves and in others, is essential for civilised discussion. Utilitarian thinking is particularly open to the danger of failing to recognise that. Since it sets out to be capable of something like scientific proof, it heightens the temptation to believe that those who oppose its conclusions are at best uninformed and at worst bigoted. The sacred human search for truth is reduced to a quasi-scientific calculation. To approach moral reasoning as if it were a scientific process is to misunderstand what is involved and to claim a kind of precision that moral reasoning cannot usually achieve except in clear-cut negative statements such as that the deliberate murder of an innocent person can never be justified. Such precision can rarely be found in political, economic and social questions, where, as we know too well, even carefully thought out decisions can look very different in hindsight. The apparently scientific approach of Utilitarianism can lead to a frame of mind, examples of which can be found in all fundamentalism, including Christian fundamentalism, which imagines that it is reasonable for us who 'know the truth' to force those who cannot see the truth to conform to what 'enlightened' people are convinced they can see clearly.

In *Laudato Si'* when Pope Francis writes of the urgency of the situation we face, he is speaking of the danger of an ecological disaster, but also of something even more profound. He refers to St John Paul's clear call to 'safeguard the moral conditions for an authentic human ecology'.[28] Human beings should not imagine that we 'can make arbitrary use of the earth, subjecting it without restraint to [our] will, as though it did not have its own requisites and a prior God-given purpose, which [we] can indeed develop but must not betray'.[29]

Pope Benedict made the connection between care for the planet and human ecology explicit:

> ... *the decisive issue is the overall moral tenor of society.* If there is a lack of respect for the right to life and to a natural death, if human conception, gestation and birth are made artificial, if human embryos are sacrificed to research, the conscience of society ends up losing the concept of human ecology and, along with it, that of environmental ecology.[30]

Pope Francis puts the issue starkly:

Doomsday predictions can no longer be met with irony or disdain. We may well be leaving debris, desolation and filth to coming generations. The pace of consumption, waste and environmental change has so stretched the planet's capacity that our contemporary lifestyle, unsustainable as it is, can only precipitate catastrophes, such as those which even now periodically occur in different areas of the world. The effects of the present imbalance can only be reduced by our decisive action, here and now. We need to reflect on our accountability before those who will have to endure the dire consequences.[31]

The truth is that creation is not infinitely malleable; it has its own meaning and purpose. *Laudato Si'* calls for a recognition of the created world as a gift to be received, not merely as material to be manipulated without any thought for the God who created it or for the brothers and sisters praised in the great hymn of Francis of Assisi – that is God's gift of creation, human, animate and inanimate.

Chapter Four

Conscience: On Not Being Judgemental

One of the great sins in modern culture is 'being judgemental'. And that is as it should be. Pope Francis asked, 'Who am I to judge?' Well yes, but that is not quite what he said. The official translation was: 'If someone is gay and is searching for the Lord and has good will, then who am I to judge him?' Journalists and others automatically removed the exclusive word 'him' and so we were left with 'who am I to judge?' This became the commonly accepted translation. It would, however, be more accurate to translate the original Italian as, 'If a person is gay and seeks the Lord and has good will, then who am I to judge that person (or 'such a person')?'[1] The common translation might be taken to mean, 'who am I to disagree with him, or with anybody else for that matter'. The correct translation makes it clear that what the Pope said was 'who am I to judge *a person* of good will?' This would not at all exclude the possibility that Pope Francis might strongly disagree with the person's opinion, or with his/her decision taken in good faith. After all, in our own lives, we may find ourselves, in hindsight, strongly disagreeing even with our own honestly made decisions! We may, for instance, become aware of factors that we had not taken into account at the time.

That prompts the question: 'what exactly is it that we should not be judgemental about?' The most fundamental meaning of the statement 'one should not be judgemental' is that we should not, in fact we *cannot*, judge another *person*. It is particularly wrong to do so if we seek to judge them in relation to ourselves, trying, consciously or unconsciously, to show that we are better people than they are. That is at the heart of the familiar Gospel parable. The Pharisee went up to the Temple to pray and said 'God, I thank you that I am not like other people: thieves, rogues, adulterers, or even like this tax-collector', but he was not the one who went home justified (Luke 18:11). The Pharisee was judgemental. He thought he could look down on the tax collector as morally inferior. But the truth was that the tax collector was superior to him in what really mattered: that is, in understanding the nature of his relationship with God who is merciful love.

Only God can judge the heart of a person. No one can judge him or herself, still less can one judge someone else. The *Catechism of the Catholic Church* says: 'The heart is our hidden centre, beyond the grasp of our reason and of others; only the Spirit of God can fathom the human heart and know it fully.'[2] No one can enter into other people's hearts and fully understand their loyalties, their traumas, the pressures that affect them, their inner conflicts and the possibly troubled struggle that went into the making of their decisions. God sees all of that, and sees it more clearly than the person him/herself.

Being non-judgemental is necessary, but it is not enough:

> To refrain from judgement and condemnation means, in a positive sense, to know how to accept the good in every person and to spare him any suffering that might be caused by our partial judgment and our presumption to know everything about him. But this is still not sufficient to express mercy. Jesus asks us also to forgive and to give. To be instruments of mercy because it was we who first received mercy from God.[3]

None of this, however, means that it is impossible to judge an *action* performed by another person. It must be possible in some cases to say, 'whatever was going on in your inner heart, whatever the depth of sincerity which may render you entirely guiltless, nevertheless when you took my property, or slandered me, or disregarded my rights. I was wronged by what you did'.

Indeed, when I look back on an action that I performed myself, I may have to admit that I have done an injustice to someone and that I should apologise and seek to remedy the harm. This may be true even though I may have acted in complete good faith. If I picked up an item, utterly convinced that it was mine, and it turns out that it belongs to someone else, I am obliged to return it just as I would be if I had deliberately stolen it. In looking back over our past, we may have to realise in many cases that, if I had seen the situation then with the clarity with which I see it now, I would have recognised that I was making the wrong choice.

The difference between judging a person and judging an action is crucial. To say that I must not judge a person cannot mean that I must agree with every choice that person has made, or that I must endorse all the convictions the person has.

People's conscientious convictions arise from their search for the truth, which, as St John Paul expressed it, is ultimately also their search for God.[4] For this reason, I should treat another person's searching and conclusions with respect, even reverence. To begin from the assumption that somebody's opinion is not worth listening to, or that his or her search has not been honest and sincere, would certainly be disrespectful. But one cannot conclude that it is disrespectful for person A to disagree with person B's convictions, even his/her most deeply held convictions. That would lead to the absurd conclusion that B's beliefs should be treated with respect, but A's different beliefs should be dismissed as disrespectful. And, of course, vice versa!

Although the contradiction is obvious, one can easily see how this situation can arise. If a person's choices in the area of religion or politics or social policy or personal relationships are held with deep conviction, it is understandable that he or she may see any disagreement with these choices or convictions as a rejection of him or herself. It is important to recognise that, however understandable this may be, a situation where disagreement becomes indistinguishable from personal rejection would make rational, respectful dialogue impossible.

There can be further breakdown when one person involved in a disagreement yields to the temptation to attribute hostile motives or ingrained prejudices to the other. It is a temptation that we all feel. When someone cannot see things that seem obvious and important to us we are tempted to think that they must be blind, or prejudiced or moved by unworthy motives. On some occasions, it might, in reality, be the case that the other person *is* hostile and unreasonable. It may, also be the case that it is we ourselves who are prejudiced. Civilised discussion should begin from the presumption that all concerned are honestly seeking the truth. Only if it becomes undeniably clear that a person is not ready to engage in mutually respectful dialogue should one reluctantly, and with continued respect for the other person, conclude that no purpose can be served, at least for the moment, by continuing the discussion. Nor should we exclude the possibility that some or all of the blame for the breakdown may lie with ourselves! It should never mean making a judgement which denies the dignity of the person who disagrees with us.

Without mutual respect there can be no tolerant or plural society. For someone to say, 'I find myself in disagreement with your position', is not a denial of respect for that person. Such a view even if strongly professed and even if the disagreement is fundamental, may be simply a legitimate expression of one's convictions. It may even be an expression of respect to be honest enough to tell someone, 'I think you are making a mistake'. That is not to say that it might not be unwise, inopportune, or discourteous to express one's failings in a particular situation. There are contexts where 'a Christian knows when it is time to speak of God and when it is better to say nothing and to let love alone speak'.[5]

If, however, one's position is expressed in a way that suggests that the person concerned and his or her convictions are not to be taken seriously, that is an entirely different matter. There we begin to move into the realm of prejudice, that is, of a negative judgement on *the person*, or the group to which he or she belongs.

Saint Thomas Aquinas, in the *Summa Theologiae*, always presents opinions contrary to his own as forcefully as he can. He lists them without rancour under the heading of Objection*s*. Invariably, 'he seeks to find the grains of truth even in very different positions to his own.'[6]

We should remain open to recognising the elements of truth that are present in the convictions of someone we disagree with. There are few if any honest expressions of opinion in which there is no grain of truth to be found. These grains may provide the basis for a future growth in understanding. Honest convictions are the fruit of a search for truth and for God, the search in which those on both sides of the argument are involved.

We need also to remain open to understanding and appreciating the experiences, cultural background and beliefs that have led to convictions that differ from ours and to the strength with which they are held. Understanding, as the phrase has it, 'where the other is coming from' may lead some of the way towards mutual understanding.

Conscience and obeying the law

Saint John Paul II said that, 'Objectively speaking, the search for truth and the search for God are one and the same.'[7] It follows that when we are faced with a person's conscientious convictions, we are dealing with something sacred. Respect means that I must not belittle or dismiss those convictions but must rather regard them as an expression of something that is fundamental to our common human dignity: that we are beings who seek the truth.[8]

No one should be obliged by law or by any kind of coercion to act as if they did not believe their conscientious convictions to be true.

A society that seeks to oblige citizens to act against what they believe to be right risks undermining the basis of its own legitimacy. Society, after all, is built on its citizens' convictions about truth and justice and human dignity.

Hence the great danger of political parties seeking to put pressure on politicians as to how they should vote on what are clearly issues of conscience. The fact that such a denial is the norm in Ireland is a sign of weak respect for the conscientious convictions of politicians, and it is an acceptance that it is normal for public representatives to vote contrary to their convictions. When this happens on matters of principle, the foundation of the integrity and credibility of politics is weakened. Many issues of economic and social policy are not of this kind, since the impact of particular decisions is often quite unpredictable and there is room for uncertainty and difference of opinion about which decision would be best.

The human rights of another person demand, not that I agree with him/her, not that I associate myself with that person's belief, but that I do not deny a person's right to hold their convictions and to express them with due respect to those who disagree. Nor should an individual be compelled to express convictions that he or she does not hold.

There is an important distinction to be made between preventing people from doing what they believe they should be allowed to do, and coercing people into doing what they believe to be wrong. We can envisage situations where it may be necessary to prevent people from doing what they believe they should be allowed to do, where doing so would violate other people's rights. If a person believes that it is his or her right to drive home when drunk, to express hatred and threats to people of other races or beliefs, society may rightly judge that it is right and necessary, to prevent such actions.

Coercing someone into doing when they believe to be wrong, on the other hand, means requiring that person directly to violate his or her conscience.

It would be ironic if a legal provision which is presented as being simply about respecting the right of people to do what they believe to be right, should be used to coerce other people into doing what they believe to be wrong!

Conscience and legalism

In a very interesting lecture on the subject of conscience, the then Cardinal Ratzinger reflected about a remark of one of his academic colleagues who expressed the view that we should be grateful to God who was so merciful as to leave many people in a state of non-belief.[9] This meant that they could, in good conscience, do all sorts of things that are forbidden by Christian morality.

This is a profound misunderstanding which derives from a legalism that was characteristic of a certain kind of Catholicism prior to Vatican II, which may still survive in some situations. The future Benedict XVI asks whether that kind of legalism can really be an encounter with truth and whether, the truth is not rather to be found 'in the overcoming of such legalism'. Legalism can lead to a serious distortion which ends up thinking, 'If the Church doesn't have a rule about this it means I can do whatever I like.' Such a morality would be childish. Obedience is not the only, nor even the most important, virtue. The fundamental moral obligation is not obedience but love – a love which implies seeking to be in harmony with the plan of God who is infinite love and truth and beauty. Obedience to rules cannot be the overriding virtue:

> An adult who was obedient in his whole manner of living, in all his acts, no matter whether they were connected with sexual or civic matters, would be unworthy of the name of man. One could consider him only as a being degraded to a state most adequately to be described as infantile.[10]

The vision of conscience in the remark of Cardinal Ratzinger's colleague, saw conscience as a '*protective shell into which a person can escape and there hide from reality*'. All that is required for peace of mind in this view, would be to become convinced about one's own opinions and/or to accommodate oneself to the opinion of others.

Conscience is about something deeper than that. In many languages, the word 'conscience' is used in two senses which are more closely related than we might initially think. In some cases, it is used in our sense, sometimes with the adjective 'moral'. Thus in French one would say '*conscience morale*', to mean what we would call simply 'conscience'. But the word is also used in French and other languages to mean what we would call 'consciousness' or self-awareness.

The Second Vatican Council said:

> Deep within their consciences men and women discover a law which they have not laid upon themselves and which they must obey. Its voice, ever calling them to love and to do what is good and to avoid evil, tells them inwardly at the right moment: do this, shun that. For they have in their hearts a law inscribed by God. Their dignity rests in observing this law, and by it they will be judged. Their conscience is people's most secret core and their sanctuary. There they are alone with God whose voice echoes in their depths. By conscience, in a wonderful way, that law is made known which is fulfilled in the love of God and of one's neighbour.[11]

The person who suggested that we would be better off if we were unaware of Christian morality and untroubled by the voice of Christian conscience, was, unwittingly saying that we would be better off not knowing who we are, how God loves us and what God who is love wishes for us. He was looking at conscience as something that confines and restricts us rather than seeing it as a way of understanding the essence of our whole being – the wonder and amazement at human worth and dignity which is also called the Gospel.[12]

Following one's conscience

The heart of Cardinal Ratzinger's article arises from a discussion with some colleagues who raised the issue of our obligation to follow our conscientious convictions even when they are erroneous. Hitler and the SS who engaged in the horrific atrocities of the Shoah, were, these colleagues suggested, profoundly and fanatically convinced of the rightness of their actions. Are we therefore, they asked, to say that they were right to behave as they did, since they were following their consciences? Our revulsion at their deeds makes us feel sure that there must be something wrong with such reasoning!

Conscience, considered as the 'secret core and sanctuary' in which God speaks to us brings us to something deeper. The human heart is 'our hidden centre, beyond the grasp of our reason and of others.'[13] This points to a deeper level than what is usually understood by the word conscience. This is expressed in the text of the Letter to the Romans 2:14-16:

> When Gentiles, who do not possess the law, do instinctively what the law requires, these, though not having the law, are a law to themselves. They show that what the law requires is written on their hearts, to which their own conscience also bears witness; and their conflicting thoughts will accuse or perhaps excuse them on the day when, according to my gospel, God, through Jesus Christ, will judge the secret thoughts of all.

Sometimes people misunderstand the meaning of 'natural law', thinking of it as some kind of dusty tome containing a set of rigid rules. It refers to the law 'written' in our hearts, which arises from knowing, deeply but imperfectly, the nature and purpose of our existence. In speaking about this deeper level, Cardinal Ratzinger referred to St Basil's phrase, 'the spark of divine love which has been hidden in us'.[14] This presence of God is not a set of rules. It is a deep memory of God's word of invitation which was spoken to us at our coming into existence and which remains always echoing in our hearts. This guiding presence of God within us, which invites us to respond, was sometimes called *synderesis*.[15] Cardinal Ratzinger preferred to call it *anamnesis* by which he means a profound memory of our having been called by God:

> This memory [anamnesis] of the origin, which results from the fact that our being is made in the image of God, is not a conceptually articulated knowing, a store

Conscience: On Not Being Judgemental | 73

of contents waiting to be brought forth. It is so to speak an inner sense, a capacity to recall, so that the one whom it addresses, if he or she is not inwardly self-absorbed, is able to recognise its echo from within and say: 'That's it! That's what my nature points to and seeks.'

This means, first of all, that conscience is not imposed by some alien, outside force. It is the sense of a love, truth and goodness from which our existence comes and which our lives are meant to reflect. Our ultimate goal is that love, truth and goodness which is reflected in our own deepest reality. The true meaning of the moral teaching of the Church is to be the advocate of this Christian memory of God who has spoken, and continues to speak in the heart of each of us. It is that invitation that gives us our hope, our dignity and our identity as sharers in the life of God.

The invitation to converse with God is addressed to [the human being] as soon as he comes into existence. For if man exists it is because God has created him through love, and through love continues to hold him in existence.[16]

Cardinal Ratzinger puts it like this:

It is never wrong to follow the convictions one has arrived at – in fact, one must do so. But it can very well be wrong to have come to such askew convictions in the first place, by having stifled the protest of the anamnesis of being. The

> guilt lies then in a different place, much deeper – not in the present act, not in the present judgment of conscience but in the neglect of my being which made me deaf to the internal promptings of truth. For this reason, even the criminals [like Hitler and Stalin] who act out of conviction remain guilty. These crass examples should not serve to put us at ease but should rouse us to take seriously the earnestness of the plea: 'Free me from my unknown guilt' (Ps 19:13).

Deep in the heart of even the most fanatical of people, carrying out the most ruthless deeds, there is a protest, however determinedly it may have been stifled, against the rejection of 'the internal promptings of truth'.

The colleague who spoke of how people might be happier without the burden of God's demands was no doubt unaware that he was echoing the Grand Inquisitor in Dostoyevsky's *Brothers Karamazov*. The Inquisitor interrogated Jesus, returned to earth, criticising him for presenting a message too hard for 'ordinary' people to follow. We have, he admits, 'yielded to the temptations you rejected in the desert so as to give people miracles, mystery and authority. It's not your message that we are giving them, it will not bring them salvation, but it keeps them happy'.

Only the truth can set us free. To discover the truth, about God, about ourselves, about the dignity of our brothers and sisters, about the creation which is God's gift to us, is our first moral goal. That can be a difficult task.

The search for truth about decisions we face can all too easily become a search for reasons to justify what we want to do. A genuine search for truth involves seeking what is deepest within us, the call of God. The seriousness and the challenge of that task is eloquently indicated in the words of Karl Rahner when he describes the moment when we will finally see the depths of our own selves:

> The judgement of God will uncover the hidden recesses of our heart and will confound mere introspection; while our heart will admit that at bottom it always knew what now comes to light. This knowledge was indeed knowledge of myself and therefore could not be clarified by subjective reflection. It is only when a man has turned to God that this clear knowledge, which eludes all introspection, emerges clearly and compellingly.[17]

We will not see only things that we are ashamed of, we will also see how, from the first invitation of God until the moment we stand before him, God our Father has been speaking to us, the Risen Jesus, Son of the Father, has been drawing us to himself, Holy Spirit has been praying within us with sighs too deep for words, because we did not know how to pray as we ought.

At the more accessible level, we may indeed fail to see, or we may have blinded ourselves or convinced ourselves otherwise, but the protest that comes from knowing that this is not an echo of God's invitation deep within. At some deep level, however obscurely, I know who I am.

> [The sense of sin] is linked to the sense of God, since it derives from [a person's] conscious relationship with God as his Creator, Lord and Father. Hence, just as it is impossible to eradicate completely the sense of God or to silence the conscience completely, so the sense of sin is never completely eliminated.[18]

Chapter Five

What is the Question?

At the level where we seek to make practical decisions, it is important that we ask ourselves the right questions. One might begin from the statement of Jesus in St Matthew's Gospel, in which he quotes from the great prayer of Israel:

> 'You shall love the Lord your God with all your heart, and with all your soul, and with all your mind.' This is the greatest and first commandment. And a second is like it: 'You shall love your neighbour as yourself.' On these two commandments hang all the law and the prophets.' (Mt 22: 37-40)

Love and truth necessarily go together; loving our neighbour is what enables us truly to know him or her and vice versa. The philosopher Gabriel Marcel says that if I view my neighbour as a sort of mechanism exterior to my own ego', I will miss what is most important about that person. He goes on:

> This means – and there is nothing which is more important to keep in view – that the knowledge of an individual being cannot be separated from the act of love or charity by which this being is accepted in all which makes him a unique creature or, if you like, the image of God.[1]

This reflects the fundamental reality of creation:

> *Nature expresses a design of love and truth*. It is prior to us, and it has been given to us by God as the setting for our life.[2]

Ultimately a good decision is one that is in harmony with the love and truth which characterise God's creation. Moral behaviour is not a question of starting from scratch to redesign the universe; rather it seeks to reflect the love and truth which the universe expresses. It means being true to the various relationships which, as we saw earlier [p. 7], are the truth of my being. If I reject or distort any of these, I distort all of them. For instance, Pope Francis says:

> Disregard for the duty to cultivate and maintain a proper relationship with my neighbour, for whose care and custody I am responsible, ruins my relationship with my own self, with others, with God and with the earth.[3]

In that passage he lists four relationships, not completely separate from each other, all of which need to be considered in making a decision. In looking at these relationships, we remember that our choices are not only, nor even primarily, about achieving particular results. Our free choices are a language. They are about *doing and speaking the truth*, the truth about 'my relationship with my own self, with others, with God and with the earth'. Free choices are 'spoken' as a response to what these relationships mean; they *say* whether I am being true to what they mean: whether I regard my neighbour's dignity as equal to mine and that I ought never to deny that dignity in my choices. They *say* whether I accept that God gives meaning to my life, or whether I put some created thing in the place that can only be occupied by God's eternal Word which is: 'the goal of human history, the focal point of the longings of history and of civilization, the centre of the human race, the joy of every heart and the answer to all its yearnings'.[4] They *say* whether I accept that creation is a gift to be gratefully received or whether I see it as mere matter to be manipulated as I wish. This is what St John Paul pointed to when he indicated that freedom is not only the choice for a particular action, that it is also a decision about oneself and a setting of one's own life for or against the Creator.[5]

When I say to another human being, through my free action, 'you are not my equal', I speak and perform a lie. When I say that creation is mine to do with as I will, I speak and perform a lie. When I say that God is not the source of my dignity and is not my only hope, I speak and perform a lie. That is the first question in every decision – not will it make me or others happy, not do I feel comfortable with it, but does it speak and perform the truth? So we return to the four relationships pointed to by *Laudato Si'*.

Relationship with God

This basic relationship which was brought about when, at the beginning of our existence, God spoke in our hearts the unlimitedly fruitful word which does not return empty. We experience that word, not as a clear set of rules, but perceive it in the deep conviction that says: 'That's it! That's what my nature points to and seeks', or in the realisation, perhaps only an uneasy question, that what I am doing is not in keeping with what my nature seeks. Our perception that God speaks in us is never complete and never perfectly clear. The Lord dwells in unapproachable light. Nevertheless, because that word is the most constitutive element of who I am, neither is it ever completely absent from my awareness.

This way of seeing things is fundamental to the Christian understanding. In some respects, it is in sharp conflict with some of the assumptions of our contemporary world view. The enormous advances in scientific knowledge and technological power have led to a shift in mentality from seeing nature as a gift full of wonders, to seeing it as something to be shaped to suit human wants and needs. One must be nuanced here. Science and technology have made possible many things that would not occur naturally, such as travelling across the Atlantic in few hours or the cure of diseases which in the past were incurable or the ability to be in immediate contact with people on the far side of the world.

The message of *Laudato Si'* welcomes such advances, but points out that they will be harmful to humanity if they are not accompanied 'by authentic moral and social progress'.[6] The human race needs balancing considerations to ensure that the pursuit of scientific and technological advance is not seen simply as an end in itself, but that it seeks to be at the service of the good of all the human family.

In many ways people feel that they are carried along by a culture which is powerful, in some ways enslaving, but also comfortable. It is not easy to break out of the control of this culture because it is so powerful. What can any one individual do to counter its negative aspects? Surely my wasting of water, or driving my car, or leaving the house lights on is insignificant in comparison to the scale of the ecological problem? It is true that challenges are on such a vast scale that they need to be addressed by all of us together. That does not justify any one of us in 'taking refuge in the supposed impossibility of changing the world'.[7]

Even on the level of daily decision making, I need to ask myself how my decision reflects that invitation into a relationship with God. The reality is that all my longings and desires and hopes come from that invitation. If I pursue them with no reference to their basic purpose, I distort them and render then ultimately meaningless. That is why both the serious decisions and the small routine decisions should form part of a prayerful relationship which frames our life. Saint John Paul was very challenging:

> … it would be wrong to think that ordinary Christians can be content with a shallow prayer that is unable to fill their whole life.[8]

If we really believe that our life is a response to the love of the infinite God, a following of the One who was crucified for us, a listening to the Spirit who prays in our hearts, then making a serious moral decision cannot be a casual thing. The statement 'I am following my conscience' is not one to be made lightly. It is part of the process whereby, having entered into my heart, I decide my destiny in the sight of God.[9]

A point repeatedly stressed in *Veritatis Splendor* is that we should not see the fundamental choice (often called 'the fundamental option') for or against God as something that is separate from our daily choices. The encyclical responds to suggestions that a fundamental rejection of God could take place only in the deepest level of our being, of which we are never fully aware. Saint John Paul addresses the flaw that can disguise the danger of self-deception in these theories:

> According to these theologians, mortal sin, which separates a person from God, only exists in the rejection of God, carried out at a level of freedom which is neither

to be identified with an act of choice nor capable of becoming the object of conscious awareness.[10]

The different levels of freedom and awareness certainly exist. Our deepest heart, our hidden centre, is beyond the grasp of our reason.[11] The encyclical insists that these different levels cannot be separated in the way some of these statements would suggest. If they were correct that would, on the one hand, make our daily choices insignificant and, on the other, make our profound choices completely unrelated to our free choice. Saint John Paul insists that the fundamental option *is always brought into play through conscious and free decisions*.[12] Thus he stresses the importance of our daily choices for our relationship with God.

Relationship with oneself

That leads us to the second relationship which is implied in every moral decision – the relationship with oneself. *Veritatis Splendor* spells out some of the implications of our free decision, which 'is not only the choice for one or another particular action ... [but also] *a decision about oneself*'.[13]

Every free decision involves a choice about the person who decides. To a greater or lesser extent, by exercising my freedom, I am shaping the kind of person I am becoming. Every decision I make shapes me. Repeated actions will lead others to describe me – judgementally, but not perhaps inaccurately – in terms of the kind of choices I make – generous or selfish, honest or dishonest, kind or unfeeling, etc. Some actions are so serious that even one instance may result in a lifelong label, however unforgiving and unconducive to rehabilitation that may be, for instance, the label 'murderer' or 'traitor'.

The fundamental question that faces us from this perspective is whether an action we propose to take, or have already taken, is actually an expression of 'what my nature points to and seeks'. The most basic answer to that question is found in our knowledge of the Word speaking in our hearts, a Word we never fully grasp, but never fully forget. That is why it is important to reflect and pray and allow that profound Word to be heard.

That kind of reflection can move us from being satisfied with and maybe even complacently admiring ourselves just as we are, to love of what God wishes to make of us. It can lead to an appreciation of the dignity we have as the only creatures in the world who can seek and know the truth and can love one another and our creator. We alone can freely and consciously love and praise the Creator:

> Through the human person, spokesperson for all creation, all living things praise the Lord. Our breath of life that also presupposes self-knowledge, awareness and freedom (cf. Prov 20, 27) becomes the song and prayer of the whole of life that vibrates in the universe.[14]

None of this is a power to be relentlessly used. It is a gift to be gratefully received and cherished. Understanding this is a crucial part of learning the truth about oneself – the gift which makes us who we are.

The choice about ourselves prompts us to be open to learn from the culture and tradition which have formed us. Christian history, in spite of its dark patches, has produced martyrs and saints, scholars and artists and writers who have a great richness of insight and example to offer. People, who share our understanding of life have, throughout history, faced issues not entirely unlike ours. We are not the first generation of Christ's followers and we would be irresponsible to act as though we were. The moral teaching of the Church is not invented from nothing. It seeks to crystallise and clarify that inheritance. An understanding of conscience which would make its judgements independently of that teaching would be a foolhardy rejection of inherited wisdom. This teaching has also been enriched by dialogue with other streams of thought. An example of this is to be found in the social teaching of the Church:

> The Catholic Church is open to dialogue with philosophical thought; this has enabled her to produce various syntheses between faith and reason. The development of the Church's social teaching represents such a synthesis with regard to social issues; this teaching is called to be enriched by taking up new challenges.[15]

We *are*, however, the first generation of Christians to live in the shifting, uncertain and in some ways rudderless, culture of the twenty-first century. We look to the wisdom of the past, not to provide ready-made answers which would make our decisions for us, but to strengthen and enlighten us in facing *our* challenges as they did theirs. Nor do we look simply to conform to public opinion or prevailing ideas; *we seek the truth*. Commenting on Cardinal Newman's famous statement that he would toast the Pope, but that first he would toast conscience, Cardinal Ratzinger said:

> I would say, when we are speaking of a man of conscience, we mean one who looks at things this way. A man of conscience, is one who never acquires tolerance, well-being, success, public standing, and approval on the part of prevailing opinion, at the expense of truth.[16]

But what is the truth the conscientious person seeks in making a decision? Being true to oneself might mean no more than doing whatever one wishes. But for the rich young man in Matthew's Gospel, the crucial question was not about rules; it was about the whole meaning of life.[17]

In *Veritatis Splendor* and in other encyclicals, Pope John Paul reflected on the questions about meaning which arise not alone for Christians but in every human heart:

> What is the meaning and purpose of our life? What is good and what is sin? What origin and purpose do sufferings have? What is the way to attaining true happiness? What

are death, judgment and retribution after death? Lastly, what is that final, unutterable mystery which embraces our lives and from which we take our origin and towards which we tend?[18]

This should be our crucial question too. How can one decide how life should be lived if one doesn't ask what life is for and what it means? In the absence of such questions it would not be surprising if being true to myself came to mean nothing more profound than doing whatever seems advantageous for me.

Moral choice makes its fullest sense when it is seen as seeking the right road on the journey towards the unutterable mystery. We are travelling towards the full vision of the superabundant gift which is already present in the depths of our being as 'the quiet searching and interior prompting' that set our freedom in motion in the first place.

If we acknowledge the dignity, indeed the sacredness, of the conscientious search for truth and for God in other people, it should follow that we see our own efforts to arrive at the truth, and at decisions that are right and true as sacred. Being truthful in my relationship with myself is a lifelong task and it is my fundamental responsibility. The search which I conduct – or, one might say, the search which I *am* – for the truth and for God is my fundamental task in life. It is a heavy responsibility, yet it is how we travel towards a fulfilment beyond any human imagining (I Cor 2:9).

Cardinal Ratzinger concluded his essay on conscience:

Yet the yoke of truth in fact became 'easy' (Mt 11:30) when the truth came, loved us, and consumed our guilt in the fire of his love. Only when we know and experience this from within, will we be free to hear the message of conscience with joy and without fear.[19]

Relationship with others

We have not recognised the meaning of that gift in ourselves if we do not recognise it also in all of the human family. That is the Golden Rule: 'Do to others as you would have them do to you' (Lk 6:31). By definition, we begin by seeing everything from our own point of view. The wonder of God's creation is that there are as many perspectives as there are people – not as many truths, but as many perspectives on, and searches for, the truth. We ought to treat others with the respect we would wish to receive, because that is the truth about us: 'It makes no difference whether one is the master of the world or the "poorest of the poor" on the face of the earth. Before the demands of morality, we are all absolutely equal.'[20]

This third relationship is closely linked to the second. The words of Polonius express the truth, although, though given the somewhat pedestrian nature of the rest of the advice he gives to Laertes, his real meaning was perhaps rather more shallow and worldly:

> This above all: to thine own self be true,
> And it must follow, as the night the day,
> Thou canst not then be false to any man.[21]

We have not properly understood our own gift if we do not recognise the same gift in others. Each human being:

> ... is created out of love and made in God's image and likeness. This shows us the immense dignity of each person, 'who is not just something, but *someone* [who is] capable of self-knowledge, of self-possession and of freely giving himself and entering into communion with other persons'.[22]

The fulfilment of the gift is received only by those who have responded to the least of the brothers and sisters of Christ, created as we are in God's image, and receivers as we are of God's invitation. It is on their relationship to others, especially to the weakest, that those who are standing before the throne will be judged. Reflection on this truth before we act is a reality check. It can leave none of us complacent. We live in a world where millions of the weakest among us are now in dire need, in hopeless situations and endure awful oppression and exploitation:

> All this is happening against the background of the gigantic remorse caused by the fact that, side by side

> with wealthy and surfeited people and societies, living in plenty and ruled by consumerism and pleasure, the same human family contains individuals and groups that are suffering from hunger. There are babies dying of hunger under their mothers' eyes ... This is why moral uneasiness is destined to become even more acute. It is obvious that a fundamental defect, or rather a series of defects, indeed a defective machinery is at the root of contemporary economics and materialistic civilization, which does not allow the human family to break free from such radically unjust situations.[23]

We live in a world where a rich, powerful, educated minority views the world from a kind comfort that is utterly beyond the reach of the great majority of the human family. And lest we may feel tempted to say, 'There's nothing I can do about that', we might recall that St John Paul listed among the personal sins that contribute to evil situations, the sin 'of those who take refuge in the supposed impossibility of changing the world'.[24] Our lifestyle co-exists with this misery and largely ignores it. But how loudly is the underlying moral uneasiness allowed to be heard in the developed world? How willing are we to hear it and to recognise the intolerable nature of the 'radically unjust structures'? Do we really see – the hungry, the refugee, the thirsty, the stranger, the naked, the sick and the imprisoned as brothers and sisters *in whose name* the Lord will judge us? (Mt 25: 34-45).

There is no easy comfort to be drawn, no complacent sense that 'we are the good guys' from an honest reflection on the way most of the human race is forced to live.

The vast inequalities in our world are shocking. They should not, however, blind us to the lesser forms of injustice which can occur in daily life. To say that every other person's dignity is equal sets a rigorous standard for my decisions. I always need to ask myself whether the other has become a means to my ends, an instrument in achieving my goals. Such distorted approaches can vary from the 'defective machinery' which underlies our economy, to the apparently commonplace and comfortably remote behaviours which are complicit with, and dependent on, a world which marginalises the poor.

One clear example is given in *Laudato Si'*. Pope Francis points to 'the present model of distribution, where a minority believes that it has the right to consume in a way which can never be universalised, since the planet could not even contain the waste products of such consumption'. We in Ireland and in the developed world are part of that minority, engaged in a level of consumption which could never be extended to all the human family. Besides, as Pope Francis goes on to say, 'we know that approximately a third of all food produced is discarded', and 'whenever food is thrown out it is as if it were stolen from the table of the poor'.[25] A glance into our brown bins might stir our consciences!

Relationship with the earth

This naturally leads to the question of the need in our decision making 'to become painfully aware, to dare to turn what is happening to the world into our own personal suffering and thus to discover what each of us can do about it'.[26]

The close relationship between care for the earth and care for people is expressed in a phrase often used by Pope Francis, 'a throwaway culture'. He contrasts this to the way in which nature works:

> [The problems of ecology] are closely linked to a throwaway culture which affects the excluded just as it quickly reduces things to rubbish. To cite one example, most of the paper we produce is thrown away and not recycled. It is hard for us to accept that the way natural ecosystems work is exemplary: plants synthesise nutrients which feed herbivores; these in turn become food for carnivores, which produce significant quantities of organic waste which give rise to new generations of plants.[27]

The encyclical points out how the weakest do not appear to count in the contexts where big decisions are made and that those decisions as often as not make the situation of the poor worse. All that they get is 'superficial rhetoric, sporadic acts of philanthropy and perfunctory expressions of concern'.[28]

Our attitude to the earth should not be one of possession and domination:

> In the Judaeo-Christian tradition, the word 'creation' has a broader meaning than 'nature', for it has to do with God's loving plan in which every creature has its own value and significance. Nature is usually seen as a system which can be understood in its fullest meaning when it is seen as a gift from the outstretched hand of the Father of all, and as a reality illuminated by the love which calls us together into universal communion.[29]

Though human beings are the spokespersons for creation, nevertheless creation itself speaks of God. God provides humanity 'with constant evidence of himself in created realities.'[30]

Francis of Assisi's Canticle of the Creatures from which Pope Francis took the title of his encyclical, *Laudato Si'*, praises even inanimate creation as part of the family – Brother Sun, Sister Moon, Brother Wind, Sister Water, Brother Fire, Mother Earth. In all of these, we see the God who made them and sustains them. The Biblical tradition expresses the truth that creation reveals and praises God:

> The heavens are telling the glory of God; and the firmament proclaims his handiwork (Ps 19:1);
> Creation and human beings join in praising the Creator:
> Praise him, sun and moon; praise him, all you shining stars!
> Praise him, you highest heavens, and you waters above the heavens!

> Let them praise the name of the Lord, for he commanded and they were created.
> He established them for ever and ever; he fixed their bounds, which cannot be passed ...
> Kings of the earth and all peoples, princes and all rulers of the earth!
> Young men and women alike, old and young together! (Ps 148: 3-6, 11-12)

The first and obvious conclusion is that 'this sister [Mother Earth] now cries out to us because of the harm we have inflicted on her by our irresponsible use and abuse of the good with which God has endowed her.'[31]

But a more far-reaching conclusion also follows. If we understand that the earth with all its beauty and potential and life is above all a gift, it changes how we approach everything including our moral responses. This sums up all that is implied in the four relationships and indeed the whole meaning of moral choices. It is about responding to God's gift:

> The earthly city is promoted not merely by relationships of rights and duties, but to an even greater and more fundamental extent by relationships of gratuitousness, mercy and communion.[32]

Behaving morally is not about submitting to a demand that comes to us from outside and coerces our obedience. It is about receiving the gift of our own existence. It is about receiving a gift that infinitely surpasses our hopes, our plans, our expectations, even our imaginations. Behaving morally is not a burden; it is choosing to be true to who we are, true to one another, true to the earth and true to the Creator of All, who *is* love.

Responding to a gift is not the same as obeying a diktat. God's demands are love, they are gift and so the task of conscience is not one of asking 'do I really have to?' On the contrary it is responding willingly and gratefully to a gift of infinite love:

> Those who live 'by the flesh' experience God's law as a burden, and indeed as a denial or at least a restriction of their own freedom. On the other hand, those who are impelled by love and 'walk by the Spirit' (Gal 5:16), and who desire to serve others, find in God's Law the fundamental and necessary way in which to practise love as something freely chosen and freely lived out. Indeed, they feel an interior urge – a genuine 'necessity' and no longer a form of coercion – not to stop at the minimum demands of the Law, but to live them in their 'fullness'.[33]

On happiness

Making a moral decision, therefore, involves more than being able to say, 'this will make people happy' or 'my motives are good'. Of course, both of these are important: if one's motives are bad or if one deliberately sets out to people unhappy, that would be reprehensible. But, there is another, more fundamental, question: Is this action in harmony with the truth? In other words, does it express the truth about who I am and about 'what my nature points to and seeks'? Does it express the truth about my relationship with God, with other people and with the earth? *Real happiness cannot come from what is not the truth.*

There is, of course, a sense in which the goal of human life *is* happiness for others and for oneself. The desire for happiness is written in our hearts because we are created by God and for God. Only in God will we find the truth and the happiness which is the goal of our existence.[34] That happiness will be a sharing and a blossoming of all God's gifts. It will be the celebration of the endless glory and wonder of God and of all the ways in which the divine truth and goodness and beauty are expressed, particularly in human beings, 'the only creatures on earth that God has wanted for their own sake.'[35] We will rejoice in the great variety of ways in which the infinite God has been reflected through the divine image, recognisable in a variety of expressions of human holiness, love, work for justice, courage, creativity, fidelity, forgiveness and all the other virtues, talents and gifts. We will rejoice in that great diversity. 'Since each one will possess all good together with the blessed, and they will love one another as themselves, and they will rejoice in the others' good as their own.'[36]

Blessedness and happiness are indeed the goal of our lives. The following of Christ is expressed in those terms in the Sermon on the Mount, and especially in the Beatitudes which point the way to happiness for those who live 'the basic attitudes and dispositions in life'[37] which they contain. The Beatitudes promise the kingdom of God, comfort, inheriting the earth, mercy, the vision of God, being called children of God; in short they promise a share in the happiness that God promises. In their clarity and depth, they are both 'a self-portrait of Christ'[38] and an invitation to follow him, allowing the likeness to God to grow in us.

So we return to the idea of 'gift'. The crucial characteristic of the happiness that we aim to find for others and for ourselves is that it is the fulfilment of God's plan and it is God's gift. The *Catechism of the Catholic Church* begins its first chapter by saying that the desire for God is written in the human heart, because humanity is created by God and for God who never ceases to draw the human race to the fulfilment that God alone can give. Only in God will we find the truth and happiness we never stop searching for.[39]

An event at the beginning of the public ministry of Jesus is full of depth and wisdom. He was tempted to turn stones into bread in order to satisfy his hunger; he was tempted to leap from the pinnacle of the Temple in order to impress the crowds that would then flock to him; he was tempted to wield power over people in order to ensure that they would behave properly. Searching for nourishment and popularity and power can be quite useful goals, sometimes necessary goals, but these are not what ultimately yield the happiness that human beings seek. If they become substitutes for life's meaning they become deceptive goals that can offer only a caricature of happiness. Like everything in creation, they are impermanent, flawed and fragile; none of them can be 'the whole meaning of life'. The Tempter suggested that Jesus should treat these as substitutes for God. That is what he decisively rejected.

A vision of human life that cannot face the inevitability of death would be incapable of providing 'the whole meaning' which is the gift offered by God in Christ. Any goal that is not 'the one great hope that can only be God'[40] will ultimately face the challenging words that Jesus puts in the mouth of God in St Luke's Gospel 'This very night your life is being demanded of you. And the things you have prepared, whose will they be?' (Lk 12:20).

The approach which embraces the four relationships points to that great hope:

> Our openness to others, each of whom is a 'thou' capable of knowing, loving and entering into dialogue, remains the source of our nobility as human persons. A correct relationship with the created world demands that we not weaken this social dimension of openness to others, much less the transcendent dimension of our openness to the 'Thou' of God. Our relationship with the environment can never be isolated from our relationship with others and with God. Otherwise, it would be nothing more than romantic individualism dressed up in ecological garb, locking us into a stifling immanence.[41]

Chapter Six

Mutual Incomprehension

For the Utilitarian, it is difficult to admit that there are moral rules that do not allow for exceptions. If one thinks primarily in terms of weighing up the consequences of our choices, it is hard to see how there could be any conceivable situations in which a prohibition, however important, could not be outweighed by the dire consequences of observing the rule, or the extremely desirable consequences of violating it. *Veritatis Splendor* is unequivocal:

> In the case of the positive moral precepts, prudence always has the task of verifying that they apply in a specific situation, for example, in view of other duties which may be more important or urgent. But the negative moral precepts, those prohibiting certain actions or kinds of behaviour as intrinsically evil, do not allow for any legitimate exception. They do not leave room, in any morally acceptable way, for the 'creativity' of any contrary determination whatsoever. Once the moral species of an action prohibited by a

universal rule is concretely recognised, the only morally good act is that of obeying the moral law and of refraining from the action which it forbids.[1]

Abortion

The issue of abortion is a prime example of what appears to be a dialogue of the deaf. Those who believe that the deliberate destruction of a human life is always wrong and those who feel that the anguish of a mother may justify the termination of the life in her womb do not understand one another.

The passing into law of the Protection of Life during Pregnancy Act 2013 was the latest stage in the debate about abortion in Ireland. It reveals clearly where the chasm opens between Utilitarianism which focuses on achieving the greatest happiness of the greatest number and a moral outlook founded on the inviolability of human dignity, on fidelity to who we are, and ultimately on seeking to respond to the invitation which both brings our lives into existence and which offers us the only fully satisfying hope.

We can all agree that human life has a unique place in the world, and, so far as we have yet discovered, in the whole universe. Each human being is a wonder. We may also agree that the respect that any society gives to the life of each member of the human family, and particular to the weakest, is a fundamental measure of its justice and indeed its humanity.

Therefore, to argue that abortion is a question that should concern only 'people with religious views' or that what is at stake is whether to 'impose Catholic teaching' would be a sad reflection on the state of Western culture. How we should regard the youngest members of the human species, even before they become self-aware in the same way that we are, is relevant to everyone. The unique value of every human life is fundamental to moral and legal reasoning.

For many of us it seems clear that the deliberate, intentional destruction of human life at any stage of its existence is a denial of that dignity. Some of those who take the opposite view argue that the foetus is not yet a person. This once again brings us back to our understanding of ourselves. The life in the womb is certainly an individual human life with a unique identity, a being who belongs to the human family. The great Lutheran theologian, Dietrich Bonhoeffer, was in no doubt that the suffering and distress of the mother, while she should of course receive the utmost understanding and support, cannot outweigh the right to life of her unborn child:

> Destruction of the embryo in the mother's womb is a violation of the right to life which God has bestowed on this nascent life. To raise the question whether we are here concerned already with a human being or not is merely to confuse the issue … The simple fact is that God certainly intended to create a human being and that this nascent human being has been deliberately deprived of his life. And that is nothing but murder. A great many different motives may lead to an action of

this kind: indeed, in cases where it is an act of despair, performed in circumstances of extreme human or economic destitution and misery, the guilt may often lie rather with the community than with the individual ... All these considerations must no doubt have quite a decisive influence on our personal and pastoral attitude towards the person concerned, but they cannot in any way alter the fact of murder.[2]

Before the 2013 Act, the Supreme Court in the 'X Case' had laid down the principle that abortion is justified and is permissible in Irish law if there is a risk of suicide *'which can only be avoided by the termination of [the] pregnancy'*. It is not evident what efforts the Court made to investigate other means of avoiding the risk in the case before it, or to satisfy itself that abortion would in fact avoid – or even diminish – the risk of suicide in this or in similar cases, before it ruled that the deliberate destruction of a human life was legal. Nor is it evident that the Court appreciated the Rubicon it crossed by authorising an action which would deliberately set out to destroy an innocent human life.

This raises issues about the role of the Court, the people and the legislators in determining what is legal under 'the Constitution and the law'.

In the judgement delivered by Chief Justice Finlay in the 'X case' he makes explicit reference to earlier judgements of the Court which stated: 'no interpretation of the Constitution is intended to be final for all time. It is given in the light of prevailing ideas and concepts.'[3] If, as is increasingly the case, the ideas and concepts prevailing at present are Utilitarian in character, the implications for the interpretation of the Constitution and the law are extremely far reaching.

The Irish bishops commented on this issue in 1995, pointing out that if the Supreme Court sees itself as having the right to interpret the provisions of the Constitution in that way it is claiming the right to declare that a provision of the Constitution no longer means what the people intended when they enacted it.

In the same statement they pointed out that, although the Court had said that it 'cannot choose between the views of different religious denominations about the nature and extent of natural rights', nevertheless, in deciding to interpret prevailing ideas and concepts and use them to interpret the Constitution, the Court was in fact choosing from among the different religious and philosophical views that were prevalent in society.[4]

In spite of its title, the Protection of Life during Pregnancy Act (2013) straightforwardly states that it sets out to permit the deliberate destruction of human life:

Section 22 (1) states: 'It shall be an offence to intentionally destroy human life.'

Section 22 (4) goes on to say 'For the avoidance of doubt, it is hereby declared that subsection (1) shall not apply to a medical practitioner who carries out a medical procedure referred to in section 7, 8 or 9 in accordance with that section'.

In other words, for the avoidance of doubt' the Act, even if it imposes certain conditions, *explicitly permits the intentional destruction of human life*.

When abortion was introduced in the USA and in Britain there were assurances that this would be under strict conditions and would be very limited in scope. Experience in those jurisdictions suggests that such assurances, however sincerely given, should be treated with great scepticism.

Since the very welcome abolition of capital punishment, until the passage of this Act, no law had existed in Ireland which permitted the deliberate destruction of a human life. What we have seen in the passage of Protection of Life during Pregnancy Act is evidence of increasing mutual incomprehension in relation to fundamental approaches to moral questions. This seems to have resulted in a great many of our legislators appearing to be unaware of the significance of the step they were taking. We are faced once again with the intertwined relationships which characterise every human life:

> Since everything is interrelated, concern for the protection of nature is also incompatible with the justification of abortion. How can we genuinely teach the importance of concern for other vulnerable beings, however troublesome or inconvenient they may be, if we fail to protect a human embryo, even when its presence is uncomfortable and creates difficulties?[5]

Recently there is a growing view that where an unborn child has little hope of any prolonged survival after birth, deliberately destroying that human life would represent an enlightened and civilised act, avoiding the pain of a mother having to carry a child who may probably not live for very long. The anguish of a pregnant women, who feels that abortion is her only escape from a harrowing situation, can be utterly heartrending. But if human life, whatever its prognosis, and whatever difficulties it may bring, is a gift which awakens wonder and amazement, the deliberate legalisation of its destruction shakes the moral foundations. Those who begin their moral reflections from the principle of the inviolability of human dignity see it as an act that cannot be justified.

This is not an expression of a callous lack of concern for the mother and father of the unborn child. It is rather a recognition of the uniqueness of every life. This unborn life is a human being who is terminally ill. That is not a reason to end his or her life. Each human life is worthy of wonder and welcome and protection. Showing that recognition and welcome can be enormously demanding and even excruciating. But this tiny being as soon as he or she began to exist was addressed by God and invited to share eternal life,[6] and we can be confident that he or she will surely do so. Christians may also recall that the origin of the word excruciating is rooted in the Cross.

Opponents of abortion recognise that there are cases when an intervention necessary to save the mother may pose a risk to, or may certainly destroy, the life of the foetus in her womb. The full legalisation of abortion is sometimes sought on the grounds that a mother's life must not be put at risk. In 2012 the Irish bishops wrote a letter for the Day for Life in which they referred to the prospect that a law was about to be passed, 'legislating for abortion in Ireland for the first time'. They said:

> Those who support such legislation claim that abortion can be necessary to save the life of a mother. This is not correct. Abortion is the direct and intentional destruction of an unborn baby. In rare cases, where a seriously ill pregnant woman needs medical treatment which can put the health, and even the life, of her baby at risk, every effort is made to protect and save the baby. Such treatments are legally and ethically permissible as, unlike abortion, they do not directly and intentionally seek to destroy the life of the unborn baby. In fact, everyone wants the baby to survive.[7]

This brings us once again to the core issue behind the lack of understanding in the discussion of moral questions.

Those who tend to take a Utilitarian approach may find the phrase 'direct and intentional' meaningless and irrelevant. If, at the end of whatever procedure is carried out, the baby dies, they will think, 'what difference does it make? The baby is just as dead whether it was "direct and intentional" or not!' For someone who believes that the only decisive question is about the consequences of one's actions, that is an understandable response.

But it is far from a mere quibble to distinguish between the deliberate bringing about of the death of an infant in the womb and a death which occurs as an unwelcome, heart-breaking consequence of necessary, lifesaving treatment for the mother.

Let's imagine two very different examples:

1. A couple greatly look forward to the birth of their baby. A medical problem threatens the life of the mother – cancer, heavy haemorrhaging or serious infection. The treatment that is necessary will possibly, probably, even, as far as anyone can see, certainly, result in the death of their baby and the shattering of the hopes that the pregnancy has brought.

    Brilliant medical skill, and the prayers of the couple, result in the pregnancy continuing successfully and the child is born healthy. Far from regarding this as a failure, they will see it as an unexpected, joyous, wonderful outcome. The death of their child was no part of what they had set out to achieve, either as the goal of their action or as their chosen means. It was an unavoidable and unwelcome risk which has thankfully been averted.

2. Another case might be one where the mother is deeply traumatised by being pregnant, for instance in a truly appalling situation where her pregnancy resulted from rape. The mother may feel that she would die rather than carry the baby, and could not tolerate the thought of giving birth to the rapist's child. The anguish and pressures are very real. The point of this example is not to judge the *people* involved

in making such a decision. That is never our business; it is not possible, since we can never fully know the mind of another person. What is at stake is to ask whether *the action* of deliberately ending the life of the unborn child would be morally right. The answer must be 'no' since it would deny the unborn infant, who is in no way responsible for the deeply traumatic situation, his or her right to live.

This is quite different from the first example. Here the aim of the intervention is to end the child's life. If the child were to survive the procedure would have failed.

If one takes the moral perspective that gives primary place to what it is that the people involved are choosing to do, the latter is a case of deliberately choosing to destroy a human life whereas the former is not.

If one begins from the perspective that asks whether an action causes more happiness than pain, one may decide that the death of the infant is justified by the lifting of a terrible burden from the woman and the couple. Part of the reason one might do so, of course, is that we feel the pain of those we know and have come to love, people whose dilemmas and anguish we empathise with, more sharply than the pain, and the loss of future happiness, of a foetus whom we have never seen, even in an ultra sound.

In effect the second example may assume that the question of the effect on the unborn child may be outweighed by the relief of mother's great burden. The first example looks at the decision in a wider perspective, which recognises that the right to life cannot be outweighed by the interests of others, however compelling those interests are.

The two approaches arrive at different conclusions because they are asking different questions and begin from different understandings of the meaning of human choices. The choice deliberately to destroy a human life and the choice to do all that is necessary to deal with a life-threatening illness, while reluctantly running the risk of harm or even death to the unborn child, are not the same even if their consequence might well be.

Differing viewpoints on moral issues tend to be expressed in terms which, from the beginning, favour one or other point of view. Words can be used as opposing slogans rather than as means of reaching mutual understanding. In contemporary culture, the language of utilitarianism comes so naturally that it may be seen as completely unproblematic. In any ways it has become people's native tongue. This can skew the dialogue and even entirely block conversation.

The issue of abortion is a clear example of how the two ways of thinking diverge and how the differing languages can be a source of distrust and even hostility. Those of us who regard it as a clear fact that a human life exists from the time of conception see the description of a foetus as just a 'clump of cells' or 'a potential human being', and the death of the foetus as simply 'a termination of the pregnancy', as language designed not to come face to face with the full reality of what is happening.

Euthanasia

This phenomenon of language which is divisive from the start is also evident in debates about what is called 'assisted dying', which would more accurately be called 'assisted killing'. Euthanasia either means killing a person who has asked to have his or her life ended, or enabling the person to kill him or herself. The journalist Charles Moore commented:

> The use of language is important in this debate, and the pro-killing party is clever at it. 'Choice' is favoured. Even more so is 'dying with dignity'. Whoever thought of that phrase deserves – if euthanasia-supporters admit the concept – immortality. Who, after all, could want people not to die with dignity?
>
> The BBC now uses the phrase, unchallenged, in its news coverage of the issue, as if 'dying with dignity' were an accepted euphemism for suicide, like 'passing away' for death itself. You have to stop a moment to remember that thousands of people die with dignity every day, not by their own hand, but by accepting the course of nature.[8]

No doubt some of this language of controversy is cleverly created, though it should be recognised that for many it seems entirely straightforward and obvious. But this is not just a question of language; it is about different ways of understanding who we are. A society which comes to believe that the first moral imperative is to seek the greatest happiness for the greatest number, measured by the maximisation of pleasure and the diminishing of pain, is particularly vulnerable to the temptation to see assisted suicide as the obvious response to chronic and severe pain or distress. That temptation grows quite naturally from a world view that sees it as the role of science, of society, of medicine, and of politics, to remove whatever is experienced as an obstacle to human happiness, whether that is an unwanted child in the womb, or a disease or disability, or a life which is approaching its end. Euthanasia becomes the option when, in spite of all these resources, the distress remains. Saint John Paul, who himself knew years of suffering and increasing disability, said:

> When the prevailing tendency is to value life only to the extent that it brings pleasure and well-being, suffering seems like an unbearable setback, something from which one must be freed at all costs. Death is considered 'senseless' if it suddenly interrupts a life still open to a future of new and interesting experiences. But it becomes a 'rightful liberation' once life is held to be no longer meaningful because it is filled with pain and inexorably doomed to even greater suffering ...
>
> It is especially people in the developed countries who act in this way: they feel encouraged to do so also by the constant progress of medicine and its ever more advanced techniques.[9]

In fact, for all its scientific advance and resources, unimagined in the past, the contemporary world can be an unwelcoming place for the elderly, the poor, the unemployed, the asylum seeker or the chronically ill. The response to the issue of euthanasia should not simply be to condemn it. It is necessary to *reflect* on what gives rise to the demand and especially on the conscious and unconscious ways in which people can be made to feel that they are a burden.

It always strikes me during visits to Lourdes that it is a place where one sees how the world should be; it is an eloquent witness to what is wrong with a culture that can easily prompt people who are older, less strong or less mobile, to feel that they are a nuisance or a burden, or in the way. Here the world stands 'the right way up'; Christian faith gives witness in a world whose priorities are out of kilter. Here invalids and the elderly are given first place and other pilgrims are literally 'at their service'. Here no wheelchair bound person has reason to feel, as we so often hear them say in other contexts, 'I'm holding everybody up.'

In the experience of Lourdes one can see the basic questions writ large. How do we view the meaning of life? What do we see as the source of human dignity and value? The fundamental value of a person does not lie in how physically or mentally gifted he or she is, nor in how much the person has achieved or is capable of achieving, nor in how influential the social class or the job, or the connections the person has. The real giftedness lies elsewhere, in the realisation that *each person's very existence is a gift of God.*

Ends and means

When consequences become the primary, or even the sole, criterion of the morality of an action, the distinction between ends and means tends to get lost. The phrase, 'the end doesn't justify the means', seems to make little sense when the end result of one's choice is the only deciding factor.

Desmond Fennell's book, referred to on p.18, spoke of the end of western civilisation and its replacement by something as yet unforeseen. Significantly, he regards the final abandonment of its roots, by Western civilisation as having been sealed by nuclear bombing of Hiroshima – not only the fact that it happened, but, more significantly, because so many people thought, and still think, that it was morally justified. After all, they say, though it destroyed a huge number of innocent lives, it saved many more than that by shortening the war. This is Utilitarianism on a huge scale – an action is justified because it kills fewer people than another option would. This is the point at which such an approach takes leave of the moral thinking which sees some actions as never justifiable, or to put it another way, sees some rights as inviolable and inalienable. It is not enough to weigh up the consequences of a choice when the very action one is choosing to perform is a denial of the dignity and rights of other people. The bombing of Hiroshima and Nagasaki were instances of what Vatican II very explicitly condemned: 'Every act of war directed to the indiscriminate destruction of whole cities or vast areas with their inhabitants is a crime against God and humanity.'[10] Such a decision turns real, living people into mere instruments to achieve a goal.

Hiroshima was a classic instance of what happens when one acts on the basis that the end can justify the means. It is also an instance of how the inviolability of human life challenges the assumptions and imperatives that a Utilitarianism culture can take for granted. If the violation of the right to life of innocent people is what one is choosing to do, no result of such an action can justify it.

There are other actions on a smaller scale which raise the same questions. Modern warfare directly threatens civilian populations, and therefore intensifies the issues about protecting non-combatants. To take one example, an army might respond to an attack in two ways. It might seek to destroy the artillery or rockets being used in the attack. Doing so will probably kill at least some of the soldiers firing the shells or rockets, but may not seriously threaten the civilian population. Such a response might well constitute a legitimate act of self-defence, the clear purpose of which is to stop the attack.

On the other hand, the defending forces might choose to destroy large parts of the general area from which the attacks emanate, not just to destroy the weapons, but to deter the enemy by inflicting many civilian casualties, probably including children. Or it might seek to execute hostages from that area. The purpose of such exercises is reprisal or revenge, the infliction of fear and the destruction of morale, not only in opposing armed forces but in the civilian population. It seeks to end the attack, but do so precisely by killing and terrorising people who are not engaged in attacking them.

The two actions might conceivably be equally effective in ending the bombardment, but they are morally very different. What makes the second case morally wrong is that it involves freely choosing to kill and maim innocent people. Where that is the chosen object, no motive and no foreseen consequences, however good they may seem, can make it right.

Similar questions arise, in a way that may challenge our instinctive reactions, when intelligence or police services are faced with a suspect whom they think may be in possession of information about a planned atrocity. One must, of course, ask whether torture is an effective way of extracting reliable information. That, however is another utilitarian argument! *The Compendium of the Social Doctrine of the Church* condemns terrorism in absolute terms precisely on the grounds that 'the human person is always an end and never a means'[11]

On the substantive question, *The Compendium of the Social Teaching of the Church* is unequivocal:

> In carrying out investigations, the regulation against the use of torture, even in the case of serious crimes, must be strictly observed: 'Christ's disciple refuses every recourse to such methods, which nothing could justify and in which the dignity of man is as much debased in his torturer as in the torturer's victim' [830]. International juridical instruments concerning human rights correctly indicate a prohibition against torture as a principle which cannot be contravened under any circumstances.[12]

Looking at the foundations

A utilitarian approach leads to what then Cardinal Ratzinger called 'the dictatorship of relativism'.[13] This is an approach which is unable to say that anything is wrong in itself because it cannot rule out the possibility that an overwhelmingly advantageous result might justify a negative choice, even if it involves the deliberate taking of innocent human life. In an interview a few years earlier he had said:

> I would say that today relativism predominates. It seems that whoever is not a relativist is someone who is intolerant. To think that one can understand the essential truth is already seen as something intolerant. However, in reality this exclusion of truth is a type of very grave intolerance and reduces essential things of human life to subjectivism. In this way, in essential things we no longer have a common view. Each one can and should decide as he can. So we lose the ethical foundations of our common life.[14]

This is increasingly the atmosphere in which we find ourselves. The term 'dictatorship of relativism' reflects two things – firstly that *all* moral conclusions remain fluid in the light of the likely consequences of any particular choice, and, secondly that the tone of the debates has deteriorated. The debates have, ironically, tended to become judgemental in the sense that disagreement with another person's views is interpreted as disapproval, isolation and something approaching coercion *of the person*.

The task that faces us now is to find the common ground that enables real conversation about the issues that face our society. The risk is that, if the incomprehension is not addressed, participants in these debates will be tempted to think 'my argument is not working, shout louder', or in 'sporting' terms they will be tempted to 'play the man not the ball'.

Pope Francis made an important, but sometimes misunderstood, statement:

> We cannot insist only on issues related to abortion, gay marriage and the use of contraceptive methods. This is not possible. I have not spoken much about these things, and I was reprimanded for that. But when we speak about these issues, we have to talk about them in a context.[15]

The challenge is to find a context, an understanding of human life, freedom and dignity, that will enable us to approach such divisive issues and others like the welcoming of refugees and issues surrounding care for the earth, in a way that does justice to ourselves and can provide a common basis for discussion. One might illustrate, while inevitably oversimplifying, the two world views at work, which result in a situation where 'in essential things we no longer have a common view'.

One view sees the realities of the world around us, the traditions, laws and principles that admit of no exceptions, as restrictive, and a society which has succeeded in marginalising these factors as bringing us a new freedom to shape our own lives.

The other view sees creation as providing a structure and a meaning within which we can be free, protected by the traditions and rules learned from those who have gone before us, and surrounded by reality which we fundamentally recognise not as hostile but as a gift and a promise of fulfilment. It is a view that sees the earth, and indeed the universe, as 'our common home'.[16] It believes that dismissing or minimising the wisdom, accumulated down the generations, about the most profound meaning of the reality within which we live and act, would actually leave us less free.

Bishop Robert Barron, during an address at the World Meeting of Families in Philadelphia, powerfully illustrated what it means to say that the function of law is not to be a restriction but a liberation. When he first tried to play golf, he simply put his hands around the club and tried to hit the ball as hard as he could; the result was a disaster. Then a golf professional showed him the 'rules' deriving from the experience of countless golfers, about a correct stance, about how to grip the club, how to make a proper backswing, how to swing 'through the ball'. For the first time he was able to do what he had been trying unsuccessfully to do. The rules and traditions set him free![17]

No doubt, as in most disputes, there is an element of truth in both positions. Traditions can expand our freedom by keeping us in touch with the wisdom acquired down the ages about how to understand and respond to situations and dilemmas which we meet. Laws and traditions can, on the other hand, restrict us in two ways. That will be the case if we begin by presuming that any influence from outside ourselves, diminishes our freedom, or if we approach traditions, rules and structures without trying to understand their value. Secondly, as we know well from history, laws and authority can become oppressive if they are imposed, not as a service to human dignity and freedom but as coercion by a power which is behaving unjustly.

The laws and traditions of the Church need to be looked at to ensure that they witness to God whose 'most stupendous attribute' is mercy.[18]

At the close of Vatican II, Blessed Paul VI said:

> … charity has been the principal religious feature of this Council … The religion of the God who became man has met the religion (for such it is) of man who makes himself God. And what happened? Was there a clash, a battle, a condemnation? There could have been, but there was none. The old story of the Samaritan has been the model of the spirituality of the council … all this rich teaching is channelled in one direction, the service of [humankind], of every condition, in every weakness and need.[19]

Pope Francis is clear about the significance of that approach of the Council:

> With the Council, the Church entered a new phase of her history. The Council Fathers strongly perceived, as a

true breath of the Holy Spirit, a need to talk about God to men and women of their time in a more accessible way. The walls which too long had made the Church a kind of fortress were torn down and the time had come to proclaim the Gospel in a new way … The Church sensed a responsibility to be a living sign of the Father's love in the world.[20]

Today's culture, on the other hand, with its effort to 'redraw the moral landscape', raises fundamental questions. It can have unintended consequences which leave the weakest unprotected. Seeking to maximise happiness in ourselves and others may seem unproblematic, but it may fail to take account of our capacity freely to enslave ourselves, through addiction, through irresponsible pursuits of pleasure, or by taking the easier path when one's own wellbeing and that of others would be better served by restraint, generosity, or self sacrifice. This way of looking at things can be harmful if it leads to refusal to accept pain or risk, even when human decency requires intervention at some danger or cost to oneself. It may also fail to take account of some of the origins of such an approach:

> [The early utilitarians] believed not in resisting, but in using, [people's] tendency to be slaves to their passions; they wished to dangle rewards and punishments before [them] - the acutest possible form of heteronomy - if

by this means the 'slaves' might be made happier. But to manipulate [people], to propel them towards goals which you - the social reformer - see, but they may not, is to deny their human essence, to treat them as objects without wills of their own, and therefore to degrade them.[21]

Restoring the foundations for a real meeting of minds on moral issues is not just about seeking a moral middle ground. It is a matter of truth. In the context of abortion and euthanasia David Walsh writes:

> We come to see that it is not merely a matter of finding a peaceful accommodation of a controversial moral issue, but of gaining a sense of the full dimensions of the reality at stake. The acceptance of our freedom to control the beginning and end of human life calls into question the whole notion that there is anything valuable about human beings at all that might not be drawn into the calculation of costs and benefits to themselves or others.[22]

This should not mean any lack of understanding of people in difficult circumstances who feel trapped by their circumstances. But nowadays the issue is not just about distressing individual cases.

> Decisions that go against life sometimes arise from difficult or even tragic situations of profound suffering, loneliness, a total lack of economic prospects, depression

> and anxiety about the future. Such circumstances can mitigate even to a notable degree subjective responsibility and the consequent culpability of those who make these choices which in themselves are evil. But today the problem goes far beyond the necessary recognition of these personal situations. It is a problem which exists at the cultural, social and political level, where it reveals its more sinister and disturbing aspect in the tendency, ever more widely shared, to interpret the above crimes against life as legitimate expressions of individual freedom, to be acknowledged and protected as actual rights.[23]

If everything can be decided by a calculus that weighs up pleasure and pain, even the most fundamental right – not to be deliberately deprived of one's life – may be outweighed by the benefit to be gained by disregarding it.

There are some apparent exceptions, such as self-defence, but self-defence is not a right to set out to kill an unjust assailant. It is a right to do what is necessary to repel a lethal attack, even if the assailant may be injured or killed in the process.[24]

Pope John Paul saw all of this as a crucial element in the redrawing of the moral landscape, or what he called the 'overthrowing and downfall of moral values'. It 'relativises the moral norm, denying its absolute and unconditional value, and as a consequence denying that there can be intrinsically illicit acts independent of the circumstances in which they are performed by the subject'. He is clear that 'the problem is not so much one of ignorance of Christian ethics,' but ignorance 'rather of the meaning, foundations and criteria of the moral attitude'.[25]

If there were no exception-less norms, then there would be some contexts in which anything might be permitted. In such a situation the weakest would be left vulnerable.

> These norms in fact represent the unshakable foundation and solid guarantee of a just and peaceful human coexistence, and hence of genuine democracy, which can come into being and develop only on the basis of the equality of all its members, who possess common rights and duties. When it is a matter of the moral norms prohibiting intrinsic evil, there are no privileges or exceptions for anyone. It makes no difference whether one is the master of the world or the 'poorest of the poor' on the face of the earth. Before the demands of morality, we are all absolutely equal.[26]

In a world of forced migration, totalitarian governments, summary trials and denials of fundamental human rights, torture, wars which threaten the lives and wellbeing of children and other civilians, human trafficking, drugs cartels – the list is endless – we surely need to recognise that in all these situations if no one has rights that may not be set aside, then the bell tolls for everyone.

Chapter Seven

To Sum Up: All is Gift

Starting from the idea that all is gift we may try to express the fundamental meaning of human life, dignity and freedom – the ideas that lie beneath the reflections in this book.

Frank Sheed, the author, publisher and theologian says:

> This is what really matters, to establish the worth of the human person. It is small gain to assert that all [people] are equal, if all are equal to nothing much.[1]

What is it that makes us worthy of respect? What is special about human beings? We already possess devices which contain a range of information which surpasses any human capacity and which can access that information in fractions of a second. Enter the words 'utilitarianism definition' into Google and you will be triumphantly informed 'About 446,000 results in 0.50 seconds'. There seems to be every possibility that the development of quantum computers may increase both the quantity of data and the speed of access beyond anything we can imagine. We hear a lot about the quest to create artificial intelligence. We have become familiar in science fiction with the idea of robots or androids that can think and adapt and relate to human beings as equals.

How do such projects and concepts and fictions affect how we see ourselves? If we think of our being rational simply in terms of being able to gather facts, then computers can do it better than we. But is having facts on a hard drive the same as what we mean by *knowing*? Could such computers or robots ever really love? Could they produce genuine art and literature, poetry rather than clever verse? They, and all their 'colleagues', would be interchangeable, always capable of being replicated, provided only that their programmes and contents had been properly backed up. They could never have the value, the uniqueness and the irreplaceability that are the mark of every human being. They could never be persons.

That is the central question. Equality is a concept on which we all agree, but equal in what? Frank Sheed responds in terms of the Christian vision of human worth. We see all sorts of differences among people; we may fancy that our qualities, our achievements, our cultural heritage give us a particular standing. But for him the heart of equal human dignity is that, 'compared with the immeasurable values that go simply with being a [human person] – with being a spiritual creature loved by God, [with Christ as our brother], and with an unbreakable hold on eternity – these small extra ornaments, even if they have the values their possessors see in them, are almost comically insignificant.'[2] Someone who understood that could never say, 'Christ died for that person, but my skin is a more suitable colour.'[3]

Everything that exists is a gift of the Creator. That is the core of the most profound answer to the question with which we began: 'Who are we?' Although it is expressed in terms of belief in God, Christians do not see the idea of gift as irrelevant to those who do not have faith. In the first place, Christians believe that each person, whatever their belief or lack of belief, is the result of the same creative and loving gift. Secondly, Christians express their belief, not with any sense of superiority, but rather in the hope that this high vision of human dignity may find an echo in the hearts of all human beings. Thirdly, every human being can sense that his or her life is something given, not self-created. Christians believe that human dignity is a gift we have all received:

> The Church knows that this *Gospel of Life* which she has received from her Lord has a profound echo in the heart of every person – believer and non-believer alike – because it marvellously fulfils all the heart's expectations while infinitely surpassing them.[4]

We have unique dignity and that dignity is a gift. The endless longings of the human heart are not cruel illusions. That is so because the Creator of all *is love* and has invited us to share the unlimited life of God. That is why we have a longing for what we could never create. Pope Francis addressed the people in a very poor area of Rio de Janeiro:

> Dear friends, it is certainly necessary to give bread to the hungry – this is an act of justice. But there is also a deeper hunger, the hunger for a happiness that only God can satisfy, the hunger for dignity.[5]

The astonishing experience of gift

The expectations of the heart cannot be fully answered by human ingenuity or effort. 'Eye has not seen nor ear heard nor human heart conceived what God has prepared'. (I Cor 2:9) The encyclical, *Caritas in Veritate* speaks of 'the principle of gratuitousness'. By this it means that *everything in creation is God's free gift*. Pope Benedict called it the astonishing experience of gift, and goes on to say:

> Gratuitousness is present in our lives in many different forms, which often go unrecognised because of a purely consumerist and utilitarian view of life. The human being is made for gift, which expresses and makes present his/her transcendent dimension. Sometimes [people] are wrongly convinced that [they are] the sole author of themselves, their life and society. This is a presumption that follows from being selfishly closed in on [themselves],

and it is a consequence – to express it in faith terms – of original sin.[6]

God gave us the gift of sharing in divine love so that we could enter eternal rest and joy:

> There we shall rest and see, we shall see and love, we shall love and praise. Behold what will be at the end without end. For what other end do we have, if not to reach the kingdom which has no end?[7]

That final destination is heaven, or the new creation. Referring to the words 'Blessed are the poor in spirit, for theirs is the kingdom of heaven' (Mt 5:3), *The Catechism of the Catholic Church* says:

> [This beatitude] teaches us that true happiness is not found in riches or well-being, in human fame or power, or in any human achievement - however beneficial it may be - such as science, technology, and art, or indeed in any creature, but in God alone, the source of every good and of all love.[8]

That is the hope big enough to satisfy our quest for happiness.[9] Therefore, 'what will bring about the most happiness for the most people now?' is not the key question. What we seek is a happiness to which Vatican II pointed when it described Christ as 'the goal of human history, the focal point of the longings of history and of civilisation, the centre of the human race, the joy of every heart and the answer to all its yearnings'.[10] However much happiness it brings, a choice which is not a step on the road to true happiness with God is literally 'misguided'.

Other chapters of this book have pointed to the difficulty that utilitarian approaches face in seeking to measure in a clear and accurate way the degree of happiness or its opposite that various choices will produce. Happiness is ultimately unmeasurable in scientific or mathematical terms. It varies from time to time, from context to context, from person to person. There is an unlimited longing in the human heart that is never perfectly and permanently fulfilled. Everything that we experience is fragile and fleeting, as experience sometimes painfully teaches us. Creativity and art express a gulf, never fully overcome, between limitless human longing and the impermanence and incompleteness of our happiness, however intensely we may be fortunate to rejoice in it at a particular time.

But there remains the immediacy and the beauty of what we see around us. They are reflections of the beauty, goodness, truth, power, and providence of God. But if we act as though all those appealing realities were actually God, we place ourselves in a cul de sac.

In the desert, Satan tempted Jesus to accept comfort and celebrity and unlimited coercive power over all nations. These, or at least the first two, are not necessarily bad in themselves; each could be used to good purpose. What Jesus rejected was the implication that these could take the place of God – 'not on bread alone but on every word from the mouth of God; do not tempt the Lord your God; you shall worship the Lord your God and him only shall you serve' (Mt 4: 4, 7: 10). All temptations are ultimately of that kind: something immediate, something of this life, is seen, at least for the moment, as more central to one's life than God.

The questions with which we began

If we return to the questions with which we began, what St John Paul called 'the fundamental questions that pervade human life' we may see more clearly the importance of this reflection.

> *Who am I? Where have I come from and where am I going? Why is there evil? What is there after this life?* … [These] are questions which have their common source in the quest for meaning which has always compelled the human heart. In fact, the answer given to these questions decides the direction which people seek to give to their lives.[11]

A myth has taken hold of our scientific, technological culture, namely that human happiness can be achieved without feeling it necessary even to ask these questions, still less to attempt to answer them. Furthermore, the myth conceives happiness as something that can be achieved by human planning and effort. It is of course important that we should make real efforts to try to ensure that our societies are just for everyone, to recognise the equal dignity of all people and to make the world more human.

But if we imagine that our efforts can build a world in which perfect happiness is permanently and universally achieved, we are seeking to build something that can never be. A world we would build, no matter how magnificent, could never finally satisfy the restlessness of every human heart. In any case, so long as war, selfishness, dishonesty and injustice remain possible, no perfect society can exist. Seeking a flawless world established by us, however worthy the motives, would be a blind alley, a dead end. Universal happiness thought of only in terms of what we can accomplish could never be fully achieved. No human construct lasts forever, and no human creation could finally satisfy everyone. Happiness for all human beings, living and dead, is more than we could ever build. It can only be a gift of the Creator of all.

> Happiness is not something that can be pursued, but can only be received, with gratitude, as we receive a gift, which in fact it is. So understood, we are the creatures drawn to the light of truth, and it is only in this light that we rejoice and so are made happy. Anything less is not true happiness, whatever else it might be, or whatever else in our confusion we try to call it.[12]

We live in a 'can do' world where such thoughts may seem negative and depressing. But what we can do, whether we like to admit it or not, is limited. What we can receive as God's gift is not! That was what drove the question of the rich young man, 'the aspiration at the heart of every human decision and action, the quiet searching and interior prompting which sets freedom in motion ... the echo of a call from God who is the origin and goal of human life'.[13]

That is where we find the answer to questions like 'Who am I?', 'Where am I going'? 'What is it that makes my choices good or bad?' In our deepest selves we *long* for the goal of that 'quiet searching'. Our deepest aspiration is to answer that call, to receive that gift.

The truth that 'all is gift' is not simply a fact to be filed away and referred to when required. It needs to be reflected on and to become the lens through which we see everything. If it is to give our lives the light that shows us the way, it needs to become the prayer that is capable of filling our whole life.[14]

Consent

We are not masters of the world around us, but receivers of the gift of creation. Acceptance of reality is the first step in freedom. Our freedom is founded on, not diminished by, that consent. Paul Ricoeur, 'one of the most distinguished philosophers of the twentieth century',[15] wrote a great deal about human freedom. He saw clearly that our freedom has to begin by 'consenting' to the reality that it did not create but within which it works. He said:

> To consent is not to capitulate if, in spite of appearances, the world is the possible theatre of liberty. I say: this is my place, I adopt it, I do not surrender, I acquiesce, it is well

thus, for all things work together unto good for those who love God, who are called according to his plan.[16]

The world of nature is not an obstacle to be overcome. It is the 'possible theatre of liberty'.[17] The person who draws the most out of nature, whether a farmer or a sculptor, is the one who understands and appreciates it. If, on the other hand, one sees nature simply as material to be exploited, then as Blessed Paul VI pointed out over forty years ago, we risk destroying it and becoming ourselves victims of the destruction we have wrought.[18]

This becomes all the more pressing as we more fully appreciate that all is gift. Pope Francis sums it up:

> If we acknowledge the value and the fragility of nature and, at the same time, our God-given abilities, we can finally leave behind the modern myth of unlimited material progress. A fragile world, entrusted by God to human care, challenges us to devise intelligent ways of directing, developing and limiting our power.[19]

This needs to be accurately expressed. Consent does not mean remaining passive in the face of nature. From research on subatomic particles to increasing our knowledge of the farthest reaches of the universe, we rightly expand our knowledge and our possibilities. Medical advances and feats of engineering and many great achievements have shown the importance of using our intelligence to expand our knowledge and power.

But it is still the case that faced with any given situation, it is not enough to ask ourselves what *we are capable of doing*. We have, more fundamentally to ask what we *should* do. Otherwise we may find ourselves enthusiastically sawing off the branch on which we sit. In fact, it is clear when we look at the state of our planet, ecologically, sociologically, politically, that we are already doing so. We do not like to hear that there are limits to our power; but to fail to recognise this would be to engage in the self-deception of imagining that the resources of the planet, and thus our right to use them at will, are unlimited. It would be to ignore the reality that our way of life could never be extended to the whole human family.[20]

The idea that we could shape the world without limit is flawed. In much of our lives we cannot simply decide who we wish to be – our sex, our responsibilities, our personal history, cannot simply be willed away. We are not creative as God is, making things out of nothing. We have to start where we are: with our abilities – which we can, of course, train and develop, though not in an unlimited way, since, for instance, I cannot train myself to flap my arms and fly; with the realities that surround us – which we can use as a sculptor carves the wood: only by drawing out the possibilities already inherent in the material.

In all of this we have to respect the nature of the relationships that surround us and define us – as is true above all of our relationship with God. If we want to go somewhere, we cannot as the old joke suggests, decide that we will not start from here. The really difficult challenge for each person and for each society is not simply to acknowledge *in words* that nature is not our own creation, that it is a gift. It is to *live* that conviction. That challenge will not be understood except through personal renewal, or to use the scriptural word, 'conversion'. The road towards such an attitude is one of reflection, of prayer. It means developing a sense of our responsibility not only to ourselves, but to others, to the world, and to God. If we are to understand how fundamental this attitude is, it has to become not just a formula, not just something we think about from time to time, but *our way of seeing the world and of living in the world.*

That kind of approach will recognise that a utilitarian way of looking at our freedom and our choices is too narrow and too shallow to do justice to who we are. We need to evaluate our choices by asking whether they are true to the meaning of the multiple relationships, to oneself, to others, to the earth and above all to the Creator whose gift all of these are.

The outlook that is necessary to see life in its fullness was eloquently set out by St John Paul as what he called 'a contemplative outlook':

> Such an outlook arises from faith in the God of life, who has created every individual as a 'wonder'. It is the outlook of those who see life in its deeper meaning, who grasp its utter gratuitousness, its beauty and its invitation to freedom and responsibility. It is the outlook of those who do not presume to take possession of reality but instead accept it as a gift, discovering in all things the reflection

of the Creator and seeing in every person [the Creator's] living image.[21]

The deeper meaning

Sitting in a hotel room recently, I turned on a French channel to find that I had stumbled on a panel of philosophers discussing major political and social issues. That would not be what I would expect if I were watching British or American television. If I were watching an Irish channel, however, it would be well-nigh unthinkable! We in Ireland do not seem to see the issues that shape our society in the light of the fundamental questions: 'Who am I? Where have I come from and where am I going? Why is there evil? What is there after this life?' Questions about the deeper meaning of life play no significant part in the discussion of major political decisions in Ireland.

This book has been arguing that we cannot adequately address questions of right and wrong, of what is good for us and for our society, without reflecting on the meaning and the purpose of our lives. Frank Sheed pointed out that an educator cannot hope to prepare people for life without being able to say what a person is, or what life is for. The most worrying thing of all, he says is that we do not see how odd it is that much of education proceeds without any realisation of the importance of those questions. That unawareness, he says, 'is the measure of the decay of thinking about fundamentals'.[22]

Learning to think more deeply

In May 2016, Pope Francis received the Charlemagne Prize, awarded annually by the city of Aachen for services to European understanding and unity. The list of those who have received the award since 1950 includes the names of many people whose place in the recent history of the Continent is assured. In accepting the prize, Pope Francis, as one would expect, spoke not only of past achievements but of present challenges. He began by saying that 'creativity, genius and a capacity for rebirth and part of the soul of Europe' and pointed particularly to the rebuilding and renewal of Europe after the Second World War. Then he turned to the challenge:

> There is an impression that Europe is declining, that it has lost its ability to be innovative and creative, and that it is more concerned with preserving and dominating spaces than with generating processes of inclusion and change. There is an impression that Europe is tending to become increasingly 'entrenched', rather than open to initiating new social processes capable of engaging all individuals and groups in the search for new and productive solutions to current problems …
>
> What has happened to you, the Europe of humanism, the champion of human rights, democracy and freedom? What has happened to you, Europe, the home of poets, philosophers, artists, musicians, and men and women of letters? What has happened to you, Europe, the mother of

peoples and nations, the mother of great men and women who upheld, and even sacrificed their lives for, the dignity of their brothers and sisters?

The writer Elie Wiesel, a survivor of the Nazi death camps, has said that what we need today is a 'memory transfusion'. We need to 'remember', to take a step back from the present to listen to the voice of our forebears. Remembering will help us not to repeat our past mistakes (cf. *Evangelii Gaudium*, 108), but also to re-appropriate those experiences that enabled our peoples to surmount the crises of the past. A memory transfusion can free us from today's temptation to build hastily on the shifting sands of immediate results, which may produce 'quick and easy short-term political gains, but do not enhance human fulfilment.[23]

Of course it is true that Europe still produces many 'poets, philosophers, artists, musicians, and men and women of letters'. It is also true that some, but by no means all, of the responses to the refugee crisis were generous.

It is also true of Ireland that it has many poets, writers, artists, musicians and cinematographers. But what is, perhaps, less noticeable is the lack of appreciation of those writers who seek to write about the fundamental issues of the living reality of Ireland today. Desmond Fennell points out that there has been important and internationally appreciated work of reflection about the reality of Ireland by Irish authors in recent years, many of them living abroad. One thinks of William Desmond and Richard Kearney. In Ireland, John Waters has written reflective and challenging things.

Desmond Fennell pointed out in an essay published in 2009, that there does not seem to be a 'substantial body of work, past or present, amounting to 'Irish thought', such as one would find in France or Germany.[24] He believes that there should be funding and support not only for fiction and for poetry but for a wider range of art and creative endeavours. While Irish literature in the sense of fiction and poetry is widely and rightly celebrated, literature in the sense of 'works of thought' is ignored by the official bodies established to promote Irish art: Aosdána, the Arts Council, and Culture Ireland:

> Inasmuch as [Aosdána] caters nominally for what it calls 'literature', one might expect to find in its membership creative writers as various in kind as those who make up the canonical literatures of, say, England, France or Germany. But Aosdána at its foundation formally and eccentrically defined 'literature' as consisting of only the fictive kind, that is, prose fiction, plays and poetry. Thus while Aosdána admits photographers, it excludes philosophers, regardless of their literary merits. Because Plato and Freud created merely new visions of human *reality*, they would not, if living in Ireland today, qualify for election to Aosdána.[25]

Pope Francis might well say to Ireland 'What has happened you, Island of Saints and Scholars?' There are, of course, many reasons why Irish, national spirit, Irish culture and Irish Catholicism were not at the height of their vigour and creativity in the years after emancipation. Father Donnchadh Ó Floinn expressed well how persecution on the one hand and a less than creative response to the possibilities of freedom were a missed opportunity:

> ... the Irish Church blinked and stumbled along into the full light of freedom, unaware that it was walking ungainly as if it had gyves on: that it was, for instance, unimaginatively imitative in its building, that it had no art at all, nor any great interest in Catholic intellectual life. Even today, many of us speak complacently about the dark night of persecution; we repute to ourselves as virtues the disabilities of our long persecution.[26]

Instead of trying to revive interest in the long tradition there was a kind of stagnation:

> She had grown used to obscurity. She had forgotten how she used to comport herself in her ancient choirs; how to build with her native taste; how to fashion beautiful tools for divine worship; how to compose hymns for her children to sing aloud. So, since she had to perform her worship publicly once more, she either allowed her life in the catacombs to adjust itself as best it might to

conditions above ground, or she made common cause with her sister church in England, and being content to be an English speaking church from now on, she accepted the tutelage of her younger sister, learning from her how to build and pray and preach, and sing Father Faber's *Faith of our Fathers*.[27]

Part of the heritage that was not properly appreciated was summed up in the title 'Island of Saints and Scholars'. I think that this may well be saying something rather more than that there were lots of saints and lots of scholars in Ireland. It is saying that very many people were, at the same time, both saints and scholars. The main source of scholarship and of sanctity was in the monasteries. Monastic communities drew many people around them who were not monks or nuns but were part of the life and activity that the monastery generated.

The monks transcribed not only scriptures and sacred writings; they also preserved pagan, Gaelic and European culture. Father John Ryan in his study on early Irish monasticism pointed out that:

> An examination of Columban's works shows reminiscences of Persius, Vergil, Horace, Sallust, Ovid, Juvenal and of the Christian poets Juvenus, Prudentius and Ausonius.[28]

He also noted that:

> Since the clergy and the monks displaced and succeeded the druids as the 'philosophers and theologians' of the nation, it was taken for granted that they should devote themselves to study. Thus in the lives of all the sixth-century saints the learning of letters is mentioned as a matter of course.[29]

There is an echo of this combination of what we would call secular learning and reflection on the transcendent truth in the words of Vatican II pointing to the particular need for wisdom in our time:

> Humanity's intellectual nature finds at last its perfection, as it needs to, in wisdom, which gently draws the human mind to look for and love what is true and good. Endowed with wisdom, women and men are led through visible realities to those which are invisible.
>
> Our age, more than any of the past, needs such wisdom if all humanity's discoveries are to be ennobled through human effort. Indeed the future of the world is in danger unless wiser people are forthcoming. It should also be pointed out that many nations which are poorer as far as material goods are concerned, yet richer in wisdom, can be of the greatest advantage to others.
>
> It is by the gift of the Holy Spirit that humanity, through faith, comes to contemplate and savour the mystery of God's design.[30]

Gabriel Marcel wrote of the difference between problems and mysteries.[31] We live in an age of unprecedented scientific and technological advancements. These are what Marcel called problems, which we can set out objectively and apart from ourselves – in a test tube, under a microscope in an experiment. Mysteries, on the other hand, are questions from which we cannot stand apart, because the questions are about ourselves and involve the issues we have been addressing and the questions we have repeatedly seen in important Church documents:

> As created beings, people are subject to many limitations, but they feel unlimited in their desires and in their sense of being destined for a higher life ... And so they feel themselves divided, and the result is a host of discords in social life ... Nevertheless, in the face of modern developments there is a growing body of people who are asking the most fundamental of all questions or are glimpsing them with a keener insight: 'What is humanity? What is the meaning of suffering, evil and death, which have not been eliminated by all this progress? What is the purpose of these achievements purchased at so high a price? What can people contribute to society? What can they expect from it? What happens after this earthly life is over?'[32]

Wisdom is the ability to see things whole: the problem and the mystery, the limitations and the unlimited desires, the information about the world and our understanding of ourselves, and the realisation that reality is not a mere possession to be manipulated but a gift to be received, respected and understood. Wisdom is an invitation to respond to the Giver through the four fundamental relationships, to God, to one another, to the world and to ourselves. It is not simply the result of human investigation or effort; it is the first of the gifts of the Holy Spirit.

It is an invitation to respond to a call which fulfils our unlimited desires, a meaning that we could not create or even imagine. It calls for an active response of all our heart, loving God with all our heart and soul and strength and mind and loving our neighbour as ourselves (Cf. Lk 10:27). In responding to that invitation we grow in knowledge of who we are and what our lives mean. It is an invitation that leads to a life full of meaning. I conclude with words addressed by Pope Francis to two million or more young people in Krakow in words that apply to people of all ages:

> Where does fear lead us? The feeling of being closed in on oneself, trapped. Once we feel that way, our fear starts to fester and is inevitably joined by its 'twin sister', paralysis … When we are paralysed, we miss the magic of encountering others, making friends, sharing dreams, walking at the side of others. This paralysis distances us from others, it prevents us from taking each other's hand.
>
> But in life there is another, even more dangerous, kind of paralysis. It is not easy to put our finger on it. I like

> to describe it as the paralysis that comes from confusing happiness with a sofa. In other words, to think that in order to be happy all we need is a good sofa. A sofa that makes us feel comfortable, calm, safe. A sofa like one of those we have nowadays with a built-in massage unit to put us to sleep. A sofa that promises us hours of comfort so we can escape to the world of videogames and spend all kinds of time in front of a computer screen. A sofa that keeps us safe from any kind of pain and fear. A sofa that allows us to stay home without needing to work at, or worry about, anything. 'Sofa-happiness ...
>
> For many people in fact, it is much easier and better to have drowsy and dull kids who confuse happiness with a sofa. For many people, that is more convenient than having young people who are alert and searching, trying to respond to God's dream and to all the restlessness present in the human heart. I ask you: do you want to be young people who nod off, who are drowsy and dull? Do you want others to decide your future for you? Do you want to be free? ... Do you want to work hard for your future?[33]

It is a call to restore the redrawn landscape, not by returning to the past, but by placing once again at its centre, God's dream and the restlessness of the human heart.

Endnotes

Introduction

1. J. SACKS, *The Persistence of Faith*, London: Weidenfeld and Nicolson, 1991, p. 50.
2. Cf. AUGUSTINE, *Confessions*, 1.1.1.
3. John Paul II, *Veritatis Splendor*, 73.

Chapter One

1. JOHN PAUL II, *Redemptor Hominis*.
2. JOHN PAUL II, e.g. *Fides et Ratio*, 1; *Evangelium Vitae*, 34; *Veritatis Splendor*, 9.
3. JOHN PAUL II, Message for the World Day of Peace 1991, II.
4. St Thérèse, 'The Night of the Soul', *The Story of a Soul*, London: Burns, Oates & Washbourne, 1912; 1922.
5. *Fides et Ratio*, 26.
6. Nicene Creed, Roman Missal.
7. FRANCIS, *Laudato Si'*, 67.
8. εἰκών, eikon.
9. ὁμοίωσις, homoiósis.
10. T. WARE, *The Orthodox Church*, London: Penguin Books, 1964, p. 224 [Now Metropolitan Kallistos Ware of Diokleia].
11. *Laudato Si'*, 155.

12. VATICAN II, *Gaudium et Spes*, 22.

13. Cf. BENEDICT XVI, *Spe Salvi*, 31.

14. BENEDICT, Address in Assisi, 17 June 2007 (author's italics).

15. *Gloria enim Dei vivens homo: vita autem hominis visio Dei. Si enim quae est per conditionem ostensio Dei vitam praestat omnibus in terra viventibus, multo magis ea quae est per Verbum manifestatio Patris, vitam praestat his qui vident Deum.* IRENAEUS, *Adversus Haereses*, 4.34.5–7, earlychurchtexts.com/main/irenaeus/glory_of_god_humanity_alive.shtml

16. *Adversus Haereses.*

17. J. RATZINGER, Homily at Mass *'pro eligendo romano pontifice'*, 18 April 2005.

18. BENEDICT XVI, *Deus Caritas Est*, 1.

19. *Deus Caritas Est*, quoting I Jn 4:16.

20. J. RATZINGER, Homily at the funeral of Fr Luigi Giussani, 24 February 2005.

21. JOHN PAUL II, *Redemptor Hominis*, 10.

22. FRANCIS, *Laudato Si'*, 66 (author's italics).

23. *Laudato Si'*, 237.

24. *Laudato Si'*, 240.

25. e.g. 'Action at a Distance in Quantum Mechanics', plato.stanford.edu/entries/qm-action-distance/

26. e.g. 'All Physics is Local', theatlantic.com/science/archive/2016/02/all-physics-is-local/462480/

27. *Laudato Si'*, 237. The quotation is from JOHN PAUL II, General Audience, 2 August 2000.

28. *Laudato Si'*, 240.

29. G. M. HOPKINS, 'The Grandeur of God' in *Poems*, London: Humphrey Milford, 1918.

30. *Laudato Si'*, 233.

31. JOHN PAUL II, General Audience, 9 January 2002.
32. VATICAN II, *Lumen Gentium*, 1.
33. Cf. US BISHOPS' COMMITTEE ON DOCTRINE, 'The Real Presence...' June 2001.
34. JOHN PAUL II, *Dives in Misericordia*, 11.
35. *Laudato Si'*, 49.
36. VATICAN II, *Sacrosanctum Concilium*, 10.
37. *Laudato Si'*, 236.

Chapter Two

1. *Laudato Si'*, 105.
2. G. MARCEL, *The Mystery of Being*, vol 1, Chicago: Gateway Editions, 1960, p. 260.
3. JOHN PAUL II, *Centesimus Annus*, 24.
4. JOHN PAUL II, Homily in Limerick, 1 October 1979.
5. JOHN PAUL II, *Orientale Lumen*, 16.
6. *Laudato Si'*, 11.
7. *Laudato Si'*, 11.
8. *Catechism of the Catholic Church*, 2563; cf. *Gaudium et Spes*, 16.
9. *Deus Caritas Est*, 28.
10. AQUINAS, *Summa Theologiae*, I-II, q 108, a 6.
11. *Catechism of the Catholic Church*, 2062.
12. Cf. I Cor 2:9.
13. *Veritatis Splendor*, 51.
14. *Veritatis Splendor*, 7 (italics in the original).
15. *Deus Caritas Est*, 28a.
16. *Deus Caritas Est*, 28a.

17. Cf JOHN PAUL II, Homily in Limerick, 1 October 1979, on the role of the laity in social affairs.

18. *Gaudium et Spes*, 16.

19. Cf. JOHN PAUL II, to the Secretariat for Non-Believers, 5 March 1988.

Chapter Three

1. J. SACKS, *The Persistence of Faith*, London: Weidenfeld and Nicolson, 1991, p. 420.

2. *The Persistence of Faith*, p. 50 (author's italics).

3. Similar approaches are sometimes called Consequentialism or Proportionalism.

4. ARISTOTLE, *Nicomachean Ethics*, 1.3.

5. Report of the Committee of Inquiry into Human Fertilisation and Embryology, London, 1984.

6. Cf. JOHN PAUL II, *Redemptor Hominis*, 10.

7. Quoted in chiesa.espresso.repubblica.it/articolo/1350744?eng=y (author's italics).

8. *Redemptor Hominis*, 10.

9. *Veritatis Splendor*, 74.

10. *Veritatis Splendor*, 76.

11. *Veritatis Splendor*, 79–83; cf. *Evangelium Vitae*, 57, 62, 65.

12. *Veritatis Splendor*, 80.

13. Cf. *Evangelium Vitae*, 3.

14. *Veritatis Splendor*, 78.

15. *Veritatis Splendor*, 78.

16. *Veritatis Splendor*, 65.

17. *Laudato Si'*, 6, quoting BENEDICT XVI, Address to the Bundestag, 22 September 2011.

18. YOUCAT, 45.

19. D. FENNELL, *Ireland after the end of Western Civilisation*, Belfast: Athol Books, 2009, p. 25.

20. *Gaudium et Spes*, 15.

21. *Laudato Si'*, 97, quoting BENEDICT XVI, *Veritas in Caritate*, 51.

22. *Laudato Si'*, 4.

23. R. GUARDINI, *The End of the Modern World*, Delaware: ISI Books, 1998.

24. R. JENSON, 'How the World Lost its Story' in *First Things*, March 2010, reprinted from October 1993.

25. *The End of the Modern World*, p. 109.

26. FRANCIS, Morning Homily, 18 November 2013.

27. e.g. Morning Homily, 18 November 2013, 10 April 2014.

28. *Laudato Si'*, 5; cf. *Centesimus Annus*, 38.

29. *Centesimus Annus*, 37.

30. *Caritas in Veritate*, 51.

31. *Laudato Si'*, 161.

Chapter Four

1. *Se una persona è gay e cerca il Signore e ha buona volontà, ma chi sono io per giudicarla?* The suffix *la* added to the word *giudicare* [judge] refers back to *una persona* [a person].

2. *Catechism of the Catholic Church*, 2563.

3. FRANCIS, *Misericordiae Vultus*, 14.

4. John Paul II, Message for the World Day of Peace 1991, II.

5. *Deus Caritas Est*, 31c.

6. C. Schönborn, *On Love and Friendship*, St Thomas Aquinas College, California, 8 June 2002.

7. JOHN PAUL II, Message for the World Day of Peace 1991.

8. *Fides et Ratio*, 33.

9. J. RATZINGER, *Conscience and Truth*, Address at 10th Workshop for Bishops February 1991 Dallas, Texas. Also published as *'Elogio della Coscienza'*, *Il Sabato*, 16 March 1991. Quotations in italics in this section are from that article, unless otherwise stated.

10. G. MARCEL, *Homo Viator*, tr. E. Craufurd, New York: Harper Torchbooks, 1962, p. 126.

11. *Gaudium et Spes*, 15.

12. Cf. *Redemptor Hominis*, 10.

13. *Catechism of the Catholic Church*, 2563.

14. BASIL THE GREAT, Rule for Monks (resp. 2, 1: PG 31, 908–910.)

15. This word is used in scholastic philosophy to refer to an innate capacity to apprehend the basic principles of morality. It may be a corruption of the Greek word *syneidesis*, meaning 'knowledge within'.

16. BENEDICT XVI, General Audience, 14 November 2012, cf. *Gaudium et Spes*, 19.

17. K. RAHNER, *On Prayer*, Collegeville: Liturgical Press, 1993, p. 113.

18. JOHN PAUL II, *Reconciliatio et Paenitentia*, 18.

Chapter Five

1. *Homo Viator*, pp. 23, 24.

2. *Caritas in Veritate*, 48.

3. *Laudato Si'*, 70.

4. *Gaudium et Spes*, 45.

5. Cf. *Veritatis Splendor*, 65.

6. *Laudato Si'*, 4; cf. *Gaudium et Spes*, 15.

7. *Reconciliatio et Paenitentia*, 16.

8. JOHN PAUL II, *Novo Millennio Ineunte*, 34.

9. Cf. *Gaudium et Spes*, 14.

10. *Veritatis Splendor*, 69.

11. Cf. *Catechism of the Catholic Church*, 2563.

12. *Veritatis Splendor*, 67.

13. *Veritatis Splendor*, 65 (italics in the original).

14. JOHN PAUL II, General Audience, 9 January 2002.

15. *Laudato Si'*, 63.

16. J. RATZINGER, *Conscience and Truth*, 10th Workshop for Bishops February 1991 Dallas, Texas; cf. also *Elogio della Conscienza*, Il Sabato, 16 March 1991.

17. Cf. *Veritatis Splendor*, 7.

18. *Veritatis Splendor*, 30; cf. *Redemptor Hominis*, 10; *Fides et Ratio*, 1.

19. *Conscience and Truth*.

20. *Veritatis Splendor*, 96.

21. SHAKESPEARE, *Hamlet*, Act 1, Scene 3.

22. *Laudato Si'*, 65.

23. *Dives in Misericordia*, 11.

24. *Reconciliatio et Paenitentia*, 16.

25. *Laudato Si'*, 50.

26. *Laudato Si',* 19.

27. *Laudato Si',* 22.

28. *Laudato Si'*, 54.

29. *Laudato Si'*, 76.

30. *Catechism of the Catholic Church*, 54.

31. *Laudato Si'*, 2.

32. *Caritas in Veritate*, 6.

33. *Veritatis Splendor*, 78.

34. Cf. *Catechism of the Catholic Church*, 27.
35. *Gaudium et Spes*, 24.
36. AQUINAS, *Collationes super Credo in Deum*, 12.
37. *Veritatis Splendor*, 16.
38. *Veritatis Splendor*, 16.
39. Cf. *Catechism of the Catholic Church*.
40. BENEDICT XVI, *Spe Salvi*, 31.
41. *Laudato Si'*, 119.

Chapter Six

1. *Veritatis Splendor*, 67.
2. D. BONHOEFFER, *Ethics*, Collins, 1964, p. 175.
3. Quoting J. Walsh in McGee v Attorney General [1974].
4. IRISH BISHOPS CONFERENCE, *On Civil Law and the Right to Life*, 30 June 1995.
5. *Laudato Si'*, 120.
6. Cf. *Gaudium et Spes*, 19 ('*Ad colloquium cum Deo iam inde ab ortu suo invitatur homo*').
7. IRISH BISHOPS' CONFERENCE, *Choose Life!*, 2012.
8. C. MOORE, 'If "dying with dignity" is legalised, soon it will be expected', *The Daily Telegraph*, 4 July 2014.
9. *Evangelium Vitae*, 64.
10. *Gaudium et Spes*, 80.
11. *Compendium of the Social Doctrine of the Church*, 514.
12. *Compendium of the Social Doctrine of the Church*, 404; cf. also BENEDICT XVI, Address to 12th World Congress of International Commission of Prison Pastoral Care.

13. Homily of His Eminence Card. J. Ratzinger, 18 April 2005, J. DESMOND, 'Doublethink: When an Attack on Speech Reflects Diversity', *National Catholic Register*, 17 April 2014.

14. J. RATZINGER, Interview, Murcia, Spain, 1 December 2002.

15. FRANCIS, Interview, *Civilta Cattolica*, 30 September 2013.

16. FRANCIS, *Laudato Si*,' 1, *et passim*.

17. R. BARRON, 'Living as the Image of God: Created for Joy and Love', World Meeting of Families, Philadelphia, 22 September 2015.

18. JOHN PAUL II, *Dives in Misericordia*, 13.

19. PAUL VI, Address at the final session of the Council, 7 December 1965.

20. *Misericordiae Vultus*, 4.

21. I. BERLIN, 'Two Concepts of Liberty', *Four Essays on Liberty*, Oxford: Oxford University Press, 1969, p. 11.

22. D. WALSH, *The Growth of the Liberal Soul*, Columbia: University of Missouri Press, 1997, p. 306.

23. *Evangelium Vitae*, 18.

24. Cf. *Catechism of the Catholic Church*, 2263.

25. *Reconciliatio et Paenitentia*, 18.

26. *Veritatis Splendor*, 96.

Chapter Seven

1. F. SHEED, *Society and Sanity*, London: Sheed and Ward, 1953, p. 188.

2. *Society and Sanity*, 39.

3. Cf. *Society and Sanity*, 33.

4. *Evangelium Vitae*, 2.

5. FRANCIS, Visit to the community of Varginha, 25 July 2013.

6. *Caritas in Veritate*, 34.

7. ST AUGUSTINE, *De Civitate Dei*, 22, 30, 5; cf. *Catechism of the Catholic Church* [CCC], 1720.

8. CCC, 1723.
9. Cf. BENEDICT XVI, *Spe Salvi*, 31.
10. *Gaudium et Spes*, 45.
11. *Fides et Ratio*, 1.
12. C. STAPLES, 'Pursuing True Happiness in a World without Truth', *Crisis Magazine*, 28 August 2015.
13. *Veritatis Splendor*, 7.
14. Cf. JOHN PAUL II, *Novo Millennio Ineunte*, 34.
15. plato.stanford.edu/entries/ricoeur/
16. P. RICOEUR, *Le Volontaire et L'Involontaire, Philosophie de la Volonté vol I*, Paris, 1949, p. 439 (author's translation).
17. See Chapter 3, 'Nature and Freedom'.
18. Cf. PAUL VI, *Octogesima Adveniens*, 21.
19. *Laudato Si'*, 78.
20. Cf. *Laudato Si'*, 50.
21. JOHN PAUL II, *Evangelium Vitae*, 83.
22. *Society and Sanity*, 1953, pp. 3–4.
23. Speech on accepting the Charlemagne Prize, Rome, 6 May 2016; cf. *Evangelii Gaudium*, 223, 224.
24. D. FENNELL, *On Thinking in Ireland*, desmondfennell.com/essay-on-thinking-in-ireland.htm
25. *On Thinking in Ireland.*
26. D. O'FLOINN, *The Integral Irish Tradition*, Dublin: Gill, 1955, p. 4.
27. *The Integral Irish Tradition*, p. 4.
28. J. RYAN, *Irish Monasticism, Origins and Early Development*, Dublin & Cork, 1931, p. 381.
29. *Irish Monasticism*, p. 376.

30. *Gaudium et Spes*, 15; cf. *Fides et Ratio*, 1; *Evangelium Vitae*, 34; *Veritatis Splendor*, 9.
31. G. MARCEL, *The Mystery of Being*, vol 1, Chicago, 1960, p. 260.
32. *Gaudium et Spes*, 10.
33. FRANCIS, Vigil World Youth Day, Krakow, 30 July 2016.